The Spy Who Thrilled Us

The Spy Who Thrilled Us

A Guide to the Best of the Cinematic James Bond

MICHAEL DI LEO

LIMELIGHT EDITIONS
NEW YORK

First Limelight Edition   November 2002

Copyright © 2002 by Michael Di Leo

All rights reserved under International and
Pan-American Copyright Conventions.
Published by Proscenium Publishers Inc., New York.

Manufactured in the United States of America.

Interior design by Rachel Reiss.

Library of Congress Cataloging-in-Publication Data

Di Leo, Michael, 1967-
 The spy who thrilled us : a guide to the best of the cinematic
James Bond / Michael Di Leo.--1st Limelight ed.
     p.   cm.
 ISBN 0-87910-976-9
 1. James Bond films--History and criticism. I. Title.

PN1995.9.J3 D55 2002
 791.43'651--dc21

                                        2002015758
CIP

Contents

Acknowledgments

I would like to thank the following people, without whom this book would never have been written: Ian Fleming, creator of James Bond; Albert R. "Cubby" Broccoli, the man who brought James Bond to the big screen and kept him there; my editor Mel Zerman for his guidance and patience; Nina Maynard, for her superb copy-editing; my brother John, for inspiring me to write this book and for his help in getting it published; my father John Sr., for financing my cravings for everything 007 as a child and young adult; my mother Vera, for instilling in me a love of the movies and for introducing me to the world of James Bond; and lastly, and most importantly, to my wife Elisa, for her love, support, and for staying on top of me to ensure that this book got finished.

A special acknowledgment: The original version of this book existed on the hard drive of my computer at my office in the World Financial Center, directly across the street from the World Trade Center. That computer was destroyed on September 11, 2001 when the twin towers collapsed. My wife and I were among the thousands of people who fled lower Manhattan when the second jet hit the Trade Center's south tower. This book is dedicated to my fellow compatriots at the

World Financial Center, the World Trade Center and Battery Park City, where I lived and worked for many years, and most importantly to the 2,823 brave souls who perished on that horrible day.

For the world's newest 007 fan,
my daughter, Gianna Rose

Introduction

A James Bond film is the ultimate male fantasy: gorgeous women; sex; exotic locations; bad guys; guns; gadgets; and super-cool cars. When I saw my first 007 film, *Diamonds Are Forever*, in early 1972, this four-year-old was instantly hooked for life. And I'm not the only one. Estimates say that over one billion people worldwide have seen at least one Bond movie. And every one of them has an opinion on what the best film is, who the best 007 is, who the sexiest women are, and who is the baddest bad-guy. On Bond websites and chat rooms, 007 fans from around the world argue about such things on a daily basis. This book is my attempt to set the record straight. Under a wide range of categories, I explain what the best (and in some cases, the worst) is and why.*

This book is not a history of the 007 films or a rehash of their story lines. That's been done before. Simply, this book is my opinion of what the best of the cinematic 007 is.

As villain Elliot Carver says in *Tomorrow Never Dies,* "Let the mayhem begin."

---

* This book focuses on the 19 official James Bond films produced by MGM/UA and Eon Productions. It excludes the Bond spoof *Casino Royale* and the rogue Bond production *Never Say Never Again*.

The Spy Who Thrilled Us

Sean Connery as James Bond in Goldfinger

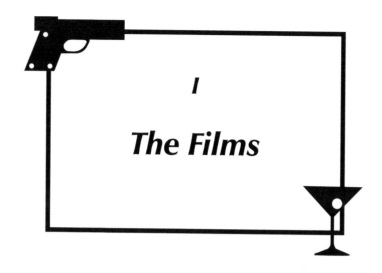

I

The Films

For any Bond fan, like me, to try and rank the Bond films in order from best to worst is a little like trying to pick your favorite children. To me, all 19 of the films are entertaining; only the bottom three are truly sub-par and even these have their highlights. So here they are, my ranking of the Bond films from best to worst:

1. Goldfinger (1964)

In the third James Bond film all the classic elements of a Bond film came together in a perfect mix-an over-the-top villain with an outrageously diabolical plan, an indestructible henchman, a sexy heroine with a funny name, an exciting pretitle sequence, a gadget-laden sports car, and a big army battle at the end between the good guys and the bad guys. This film became the standard by which all the others are judged.

Sean Connery

Sean Connery has the audience in the palms of his hands from the get-go, John Barry's blaring musical score causes goose bumps, and Gert Frobe's slithery Goldfinger leaves us wishing that he didn't have to depart this world so soon.

2. *From Russia With Love (1963)*

The second James Bond film is in many ways just as effective as *Goldfinger,* while almost being the anti-*Goldfinger*. Where *Goldfinger* can be considered a glittering fantasy, *From Russia With Love* is a bare-bones cold-war spy thriller. Missing are the over-the-top villains, the spectacular sets and the army battles. In their place is a cool, sexy, tension-building drama that crescendoes on board the famed Orient Express, when Bond and SPECTRE assassin Red Grant battle to the death in one of the best fight scenes ever filmed. This film definitely departs from what would become the standard Bond formula, but its clever story and full spectrum of interesting good guys and villains make it a film to remember.

3. *On Her Majesty's Secret Service (1969)*

The producers of the sixth Bond film did away with the gadget-ridden set-piece formula of the previous film, *You Only Live Twice*, and turned to a more realistic, human story for it and the movie most closely resembles the Ian Fleming

George Lazenby

novel on which it is based. This approach results in a slam-bang action thriller with an emotional center not seen in any other Bond film. It is the only one in which Bond gets married and loses his wife tragically in the final scene. Aided by excellent performances from Diana Rigg and Telly Savalas, George Lazenby does a servicable job. The score by John Barry is exceptional.

4. *Thunderball (1965)*

"Look Up! Look Down! Look Out! Here Comes the Biggest Bond of All!" read the promotional tag lines for the fourth Bond film and they were right. With the Bond craze persisting in 1965, the producers pulled out all the stops in this one: gadgets, girls, explosions, sharks, more girls, more explosions, and as Bond himself quips, "the kitchen sink." Every-

Sean Connery

Roger Moore

thing about this movie is big and the overall effect is mind-blowing. While it may be a bit long and slow in parts, it shows Connery in his most confident portrayal of 007, at the height of his sexual prowess, bagging every babe that comes within 10 feet of him and a climactic underwater battle that is a visual delight and Bondian mayhem at its best. To be truly appreciated, this first Bond film in Cinemascope must be viewed in all of its widescreen glory.

5. *The Spy Who Loved Me (1977)*

The tenth 007 film saved the struggling Bond series in the mid-seventies, by reestablishing the classic elements that had made Bond fun in the 60s. Essentially an updated remake of *You Only Live Twice*, it firmly established Roger Moore in the role after two uninspired turns in *Live and Let Die* and *The Man*

Sean Connery

with the Golden Gun. The wild pretitle sequence set a new standard for movie stunts. The stunts together with the Lotus-Esprit-turned-submarine car, the steel-toothed henchman Jaws, fabulous Soviet agent turned ally Anya Amasova, and production designer Ken Adams' massive and wild submarine set, make the film a veritable smorgasbord of Bondian style and fun.

6. Dr. No (1962)

The story of the first James Bond film is pretty straightforward and plays out like a 40s detective thriller; but when it was first released in 1962 it caused quite a stir. The cool, sexy and ruthless hero who kills in cold blood, has indiscriminate sex with whomever he pleases, and faces a megalomaniacal villain bent on causing havoc set this film apart from the typical Hollwood film of the time. My grandmother described seeing *Dr. No* for the first time as "un-like anything we had ever seen before." The film (a little dated now perhaps) is the perfect foundation for better things to come.

7. *The World Is Not Enough (1999)*

An emotional center and a dramatic tension give the nineteenth Bond film an impact not seen in the series since the 60s. Pierce Brosnan's third outing as 007 portrays Bond as once again suave, funny, tough, ruthless, right on target and is his best to date. But this time his Bond is vulnerable. He makes

Pierce Brosnan

mistakes and doesn't figure out who the true villain is until late in the film. Sophie Marceau is a standout. As Elektra King, watching her transform herself from helpless victim to arch-villain is the film's highlight and the main ingredient that separates *The World Is Not Enough* from Brosnan's first two Bond films. The action scenes can be a little flat (we've seen variations on them in previous Bond films), but the drama is top-notch as the final confrontation between Bond and Elektra illustrates. It is one of the highlights of the entire series.

8. *Tomorrow Never Dies (1997)*

Pierce Brosnan plays Bond with supreme confidence and style in the eighteenth James Bond film. His presence commands every scene that he is in while a media mogul's attempt to create and control world events for the profit of his

Pierce Brosnan

Timothy Dalton

empire supplies a very topical story. For the most part the film zips along at a break-neck pace; in fact there is almost too much action in the second half. The second film to star Brosnan as 007, and a marked improvement over his debut film *GoldenEye*, it's a good balance of 60s style Bond panache and 90s style super-action. And it's great to see 007 in his British Royal Navy attire once again!

9. *Licence To Kill (1989)*

To me the sixteenth Bond film ranks as one of the best for its ruthless, hard-edged portrayal of 007. Gone are the comedy and the one-liners. Instead we have a brutal revenge

Roger Moore

story loaded with intense action and drama that harks back to the early Connery days of *Dr. No* and *From Russia With Love*. Timothy Dalton's serious Bond is a bit much for many Bond fans—they either love it or hate and there seems to be no middle ground—but it fits this film's story line perfectly. Dalton is aided in his efforts by standout performances from Robert Davi as drug lord Franz Sanchez, Benicio Del Toro as henchman Dario, Carey Lowell as Bond ally Pam Bouvier, and by some of the best action sequences in this most controversial of the series.

10. Octopussy (1983)

Like predecessor *For Your Eyes Only* the story of *Octopussy* is more grounded in reality and is one of the more serious-minded of the Roger Moore Bonds. Some Bondian touches of fantasy and flair counter the serious trend from *For Your Eyes Only* and spice things up, although they can lapse into juvenile humor. The spectacular pretitle sequence, the "yo-yo" fight and a fantastic finale on top of an airplane supply great action in the thirteenth Bond film. And some top-notch, non action sequences including the Sotheby's auction, the backgammon game and the "sheep's head" dinner sequence are strong features.

11. For Your Eyes Only (1981)

Wisely, the twelfth 007 film, *For Your Eyes Only*, literally brought Bond back to earth after the eleventh 007 film, *Moonraker*, took him as far into the realm of fantasy as he could possibly go. Aside from an inane pretitle sequence,

Roger Moore

this entry generates genuine intrigue and suspense and grounds all the solid action sequences in reality. This film is by far the most serious-minded and believable of the Roger Moore Bonds and features a full range of interesting, three-dimensional characters—a rarity in a Bond movie.

12. *You Only Live Twice (1967)*

Without a doubt, the fifth 007 film, *You Only Live Twice,* is the most visually spectacular of the entire series. Eye-popping sets, beautiful locations and stunning cinematography make this film a pleasure to watch. But there is a

Sean Connery

Timothy Dalton

downside: uninteresting characters, overwrought action sequences and a lack of dramatic tension throughout. Still, the amazing visuals and John Barry's brilliant score make this a movie well worth watching.

13. *The Living Daylights (1987)*

In the fifteenth Bond film Timothy Dalton's introduction as James Bond #4 marks a dramatic shift in the tone of the series. Dalton's fresh take on the role makes his Bond more human, more serious, and more ruthless. While these attributes were a breath of fresh air after 12 years of Roger Moore's

Sean Connery

light approach to Bond, Dalton lacked that urbane, debonair quality that Connery and Moore had, and his further lack of humor make his Bond almost too serious. After the inanity of Moore's last outing as Bond, in *A View To A Kill*, Dalton's first Bond brought a solid thriller sprinkled with some great set pieces and an interesting, if over-involved plot. A little more action, a little less plot, and a strong main villain would have helped.

14. Diamonds Are Forever (1971)

Even though it stars Sean Connery, in reality, the seventh Bond film could be called the first Roger Moore Bond film, because this is the first of the series to feature the over-the-top humor that became the staple of the Moore films. While lightheartedly entertaining throughout, the film lacks the edge of the other Connery Bonds and suffers from bad special effects and Connery's bulging waistline.

15. GoldenEye (1995)

Two very good things about the seventeenth Bond film are: One, the successful reestablishment of the character of 007 in the 90's as a credible, modern action hero; two, the introduction of Pierce Brosnan as Bond—the first actor since Connery to display toughness, humor and suaveness in the role. The bad thing is the story itself. Bond doesn't leave for the main mission of the film until 45 minutes into it, and then he bounces haphazardly from one situation to the next

Pierce Brosnan

in a way that leaves one shaken, but not necessarily stirred. The noisy action seems flat. Even with some very good scenes sprinkled through the film, in this case the whole is not equal to the sum of its parts. None of which is helped by the absolutely awful musical score.

16. *Live and Let Die (1973)*

Roger Moore's era as James Bond began with the eighth of the series and continued the trend towards overt humor started in the previous film, *Diamonds Are Forever.* Moore

Roger Moore

Roger Moore

presents a pleasing screen presence in a lighthearted entertainment, but there is none of the excitement or drama of
the earlier Bond films. For a Bond film, the scope of this film
is small—unspectacular sets, rather pedestrian action (aside
from an amazing speed boat chase) and not the stand out
girls we've come to expect.

17. Moonraker (1979)

John Barry's score, Ken Adams' sets, great locations, and a
nefarious villain in Hugo Drax provide many of the quite
good elements of the eleventh Bond movie. But a continual
infusion of slapstick humor and idiotic situations that have
no place in a Bond film knocks the film off its legs. This is a
shame because buried under all of the childishness is a good
Bond movie trying to get out.

Roger Moore

18. The Man with The Golden Gun (1974)

Aside from three good things—Christopher Lee as Scaramanga, Herve Villachaise as his minute henchman Nick Nack, and the breathtaking location of Phuket—the ninth 007 film, again with Roger Moore, seems barren. Juvenile humor, senseless action sequences and a threadbare story line make this Bond film a snoozer. And let's not forget Britt Ekland as Mary Goodnight! Ouch!

19. *A View To A Kill (1985)*

One of my more excruciatingly painful experiences as a teen was watching the fourteenth Bond film on its release in 1985. After the solid efforts of *For Your Eyes Only* and *Octopussy* the series took a major step backwards in this installment, Roger Moore's swan song. From the opening "California Girls" snow-boarding sequence to the ridiculous car chase in Paris, from the awful performance by Christopher Walken and the even worse performance by Tanya Roberts to the mind-numbingly stupid fire truck chase, the film is more Keystone Cops than Bond and bears no resemblance to anything created by Ian Fleming.

Roger Moore

Auric Goldfinger (Gert Frobe) holds court in Goldfinger

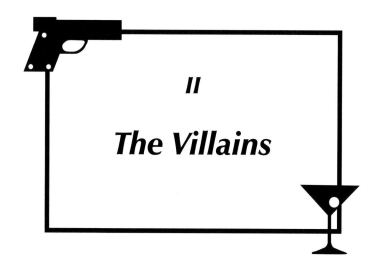

II

The Villains

Wouldn't it be great if real-life villains were as unabashedly evil as Bond villains? Whereas in real life it's sometimes hard to tell whether a certain politician or real estate mogul is actually evil or just someone who is truly trying to benefit society, with Bond villains, there is no gray area. Bond's antagonists are always mean guys who want simple, straightforward pleasures like blowing up Fort Knox; provoking nuclear war between the U.S.A. and the U.S.S.R.; destroying cities with a laser beam from space; annihilating all human life on the planet; creating an earthquake to destroy—you get the idea! Real-life villains are never this creative!

Yes, Bond villains are bad individuals, but their plans are so grandiose and their personalities so charming they seem the kind of guys you probably wouldn't mind having a drink or two with one day . . . provided James Bond was around to protect you! Here are the five best Bond villains:

1. Gert Frobe as Auric Goldfinger in Goldfinger

That the best James Bond villain would come from the best James Bond film is not surprising. Frobe's Goldfinger excels because he is so passionate in what he does. The man eats, sleeps, and drinks gold. His entire life is devoted to any enterprise that "increases my stock." When 007 foils his plan to destroy Fort Knox, we see the pain and anguish on Goldfinger's face as he confronts Bond (SEAN CONNERY) one last time as truly heartfelt. If only all of the Bond villains cared as much as Goldfinger!

2. Telly Savalas as Ernst Stavro Blofeld in On Her Majesty's Secret Service

Of all of the incarnations of Blofeld, it is Telly Savalas' portrayal that is the best. (Donald Pleasence's Blofeld in *You Only Live Twice* was one-dimensional and cartoonish; Charles Gray's in *Diamonds Are Forever* was too suave and upper crust.) Savalas plays him just right, as a conniving, cunning, sinister, master criminal. That cackling laugh he lets out during the final bobsled chase with Bond (GEORGE LAZENBY) after Blofeld's grenade has sent 007 flying off the run is priceless.

3. Robert Davi as Franz Sanchez in Licence To Kill

With Davi's drug lord Franz Sanchez we have the most realistic, three-dimensional villain there has ever been in a

Robert Davi in Licence to Kill

Bond film: a man fiercely loyal and trustworthy towards his associates, but ruthlessly vicious when crossed. Because of genuine affection for Bond (TIMOTHY DALTON), his anguish and rage are truly frightening when he finds out that Bond has double-crossed him. Amazingly enough, as evil as Sanchez is, you feel a certain respect and understanding for the man because the part is so well written and played.

4. *Louis Jourdan as Kamal Khan in Octopussy*

There has probably never been a Bond villain as weaselly as Jourdan's Kamal Khan, and that's part of the reason he is so much fun to watch. He'll stab anyone in the back—Octopussy, General Orlov, the Soviet Jewel Depository—

anyone, as long as he makes a score. Yet he still inspires loyalty in his subordinates. Think how trusted henchman Gobinda (KABIR BEDI) hesitates only slightly before climbing out of the plane when Khan tells him to go out and get Bond (ROGER MOORE). That's loyalty!

5. Jonathan Pryce as Elliot Carver in *Tomorrow Never Dies*

Pryce may be the most accomplished actor to portray a Bond villain and he doesn't disappoint as media mogul Elliot Carver. In this era of media empires Carver is scripted as one of the most topical Bond villains ever; his resemblance to real-life Rupert Murdoch only thinly disguised.

Did you know that?

Six James Bond villains have attempted to launch or detonate a nuclear weapon as part of their evil plan: Goldfinger in *Goldfinger* (atom bomb); Largo in *Thunderball* (atom bomb); Stromberg in *The Spy Who Loved Me* (submarine-launched ballistic missiles); Khan in *Octopussy* (atom bomb); Carver in *Tomorrow Never Dies* (cruise missile); Elektra in *The World Is Not Enough* (nuclear submarine reactor meltdown).

Watching Carver write his own headlines before the events have happened is a treat and his singular delight at using his media empire to shape world events adds to the viewers pleasure.

Honorable mention: Christopher Lee as Francisco Scaramanga in *The Man with the Golden Gun,* Joseph Wiseman as Dr. No in *Dr. No.*

Villain Lines

Typically, James Bond villain are articulate beings, and most of them would be damned if they are going to let James Bond get all of the best lines! Here are the five most memorable villain lines:

1. Goldfinger in Goldfinger

007 (SEAN CONNERY) lies strapped and spread-eagled on a table with Goldfinger's (GERT FROBE) laser beam unerringly inching towards the Bondian crotch. Desperate for a way out of this predicament, Bond cries out to Goldfinger, "Do you expect me to talk?" "No, Mr. Bond. I expect you to die!" Goldfinger menacingly replies.

2. *Hugo Drax in Moonraker*

Hugo Drax (MICHAEL LONSDALE) has spent most of *Moonraker* having his various henchmen try to kill James Bond (ROGER MOORE). Whether it's henchmen Chang and Jaws, snipers, assassins in gondolas or speed boats, a giant boa constrictor, or the flames of a space shuttle booster rocket, every attempt to kill Bond has failed. After the latest failure, Bond reappears on Drax' space station and an exasperated Drax, meeting him face-to-face, looks at him and says, "James Bond. You appear with the tedious inevitability of an unloved season!"

3. *Kamal Khan in Octopussy*

James Bond (ROGER MOORE) escapes from villain Kamal Khan's (LOUIS JOURDAN) mountain fortress in India. Khan with his hunting party pursues Bond down the mountain, only to watch helplessly as Bond scrambles on board a tour boat that will take him to safety. As the boat speeds away, Khan turns to his henchman and says, "Mr. Bond is a very rare breed indeed." (pauses briefly for effect) "Soon to be made extinct!"

4. *Ernst Stavro Blofeld in You Only Live Twice*

Mr. Osato (TERU SHIMADA) and Helga Brandt (KARIN DOR), Numbers 11 and 12 respectively in SPECTRE, have failed in all attempts to kill 007, which leaves Blofeld (DONALD PLEASENCE) in not exactly good spirits when they report to him and try to explain away their failures. Their news upsets him so much

Red Grant (ROBERT SHAW) confronts 007 (SEAN CONNERY) in From Russia With Love

that he has Ms. Brandt fed to the man-eating piranhas that inhabit a small pool in his quarters. As Osato in horror turns back to Blofeld after watching Ms. Brandt be devoured, Blofeld screams with absolute venom, "Kill Bond! NOW!!!"

5. Red Grant in From Russia With Love

SPECTRE assassin Red Grant (ROBERT SHAW) has cornered 007 (SEAN CONNERY) on board the Orient Express. Bond is on his knees with Grant pointing a silenced pistol at him. Grant explains how Bond will be killed and his reputation destroyed and quietly adds, "The first bullet won't kill you. Not the second. Not the third. Not until you crawl over here and kiss my foot!"

Villain Lairs

Location! Location! Location! Not only a prime factor in the real estate business, it is an important factor in where a Bond villain decides to get away from it all. A megalomaniac has to have a place to rest, unwind, and plot the downfall of western civilization, doesn't he? The five best villain lairs are:

Blofeld's volcano base in You Only Live Twice

1. *Blofeld's volcano in You Only Live Twice*

This hideout is built into the caldera of a volcano and covered by a phony lake across its crater to fool any curious onlookers. Inside are such necessary amenities as a space capsule launching pad, a monorail system to get around, and a comfy apartment complete with piranha-infested pond running through the middle of it. To keep away visitors, the crater is protected by an arsenal of remote controlled machine guns.

2. *Stromberg's "Atlantis" in The Spy Who Loved Me*

For those who love an ocean view, how about Karl Stromberg's Atlantis, an underwater city that can rise on stilts above the water! Inside: a fully stocked aquarium, a shark tank, and a team of loyal henchmen to attack unwanted passersby from mini-submarines. And don't forget the long dining room table equipped with a gun underneath to blow away any rude diners.

3. *Scaramanga's Phuket Island Hideaway in The Man with the Golden Gun*

If location really is the most important factor in real estate, then no one has a better piece of property than Francisco Scaramanga. Sited on what may be the most beautiful and exotic beach in the world, his lair includes a solar-energy processing center that converts sunlight into electricity, a carnival funhouse where guests can try out their marksmanship against Scaramanga and other famous criminals, and a solar-powered laser gun which truly allows Scaramanga to declare himself "The man with the golden gun." The entire place is run by the ever-reliable Nick Nack, a *cordon bleu* chef with a "knack" for diabolical deception.

4. Dr. No's Crab Key Escape in *Dr. No*

Dr. No must be given the credit for starting the trend of outlandish villain hideaways. His little getaway on the Caribbean island of Crab Key is outfitted with such amenities as a million dollar aquarium that surrounds the main dining room, a flame-throwing car shaped like a dragon and a large radio-beam that is used to topple American rockets lifting off from nearby Cape Canaveral.

5. Blofeld's "Piz Gloria" mountain retreat in *On Her Majesty's Secret Service*

After having his Japanese volcano hideout destroyed by James Bond in *You Only Live Twice* Blofeld was in the market for something a little smaller and in a cooler climate. He found the perfect place in a nice little mountain retreat called "Piz Gloria" atop a Swiss Alp, complete with a bobsled run, a cable-car that rides into the local village, and a germ warfare production plant. Unfortunately for Blofeld, that pesky James Bond shows up again and, you guessed it, blows the place to smithereens. Having 007 as a guest is not good for property values.

Villains Killing Their Own

We know the villains in Bond films do spend a lot of time trying to kill Bond, with no success. But there are times when to keep order or mete out punishment, villains must resort to killing their associates. In this they have been very successful, although seeing they are James Bond villains, they cannot kill people in any ordinary fashion. Something more creative is needed. Here are the five best examples of "villains killing their own."

1. Blofeld sinking Helga Brandt in You Only Live Twice

Helga Brandt (KARIN DOR), SPECTRE Number 12, has just informed Ernst Stavro Blofeld (DONALD PLEASENCE), SPECTRE Number 1, that she has failed in her attempt to kill James Bond (SEAN CONNERY). Blofeld excuses her and she begins to leave his apartment. To do so, she must walk over an arched metal footbridge that spans a small pool that runs through Blofeld's hideaway. As she gets halfway across, Blofeld steps on a pedal beneath his desk that causes the bridge to collapse, and Helga plunges into the water. Before she can swim out, she is attacked by man-eating piranhas that quickly devour the poor woman to the bone.

2. *Goldfinger disposing of Mr. Solo in Goldfinger*

One of Auric Goldfinger's partners, the American gangster known as Mr. Solo (MARTIN BENSON), has just informed Goldfinger (GERT FROBE) that he wants no part in Goldfinger's plan to "rob" Fort Knox. He demands to be taken to the airport immediately. Goldfinger obliges by dispatching his trusty manservant Odd Job (HAROLD SAKATA) to drive Solo there. The gold bullion that Goldfinger owes Solo is loaded in the trunk of the car and Odd Job and Solo take off for the airport. Halfway there, however, Odd Job pulls off of the road and shoots Mr. Solo dead. Now, I admit that's not very creative or unique. What follows is. Odd Job calmly drives to a local junkyard and drops off the body plus the car. With Mr. Solo slumped in the backseat, a giant magnet picks the car up and drops it into a hydraulic compactor that quickly crushes it into a small cube of tangled metal the size of your average cardboard box. This "metal box" is dropped into the back of a pick-up truck that Odd Job immediately drives away. Odd Job drives back to Goldfinger's farm, where Goldfinger is chatting with a captive 007. Turning to Bond Goldfinger says, "Excuse me. But I must retrieve my gold from the late Mr. Solo."

3. *Drax eliminating Corinne Dufour in Moonraker*

Villain Hugo Drax (MICHAEL LONSDALE) confronts his assistant, Corinne Dufour (CORINNE CLERY), on the lawn of his estate. It seems Ms. Dufour spent the previous night with 007 and showed him a safe containing sensitive material. Ms. Dufour tries to deny this, but Drax informs her that she is fired. A distraught woman begins to walk away. As she does so, Drax snaps his fingers and his henchman Chang appears holding Drax' two Doberman pinschers. Ms. Dufour senses the impending danger and increase her pace. The dogs are released and chase a now running Ms. Dufour into the woods. John Barry's haunting and eerie music accentuates the atmosphere as the dogs gain on the desperate Ms. Dufour and eventually overtake her. Without a doubt, one of the scarier moments of the series.

Corinne Dufour (CORINNE CLERY) in Moonraker

4. *Blofeld's prescription for Dr. Tynan in Diamonds Are Forever*

"The scorpion," states Mr. Wint (BRUCE GLOVER). "Mother Nature's finest killer," says Mr. Kidd (PUTTER SMITH). "One is never too old to learn from a master," Mr. Wint adds. Wint and Kidd, two of Blofeld's assassins, have the task of eliminating all links in the diamond smuggling pipeline that has been feeding Blofeld. The first link in that pipeline is the unsuspecting dentist Dr. Tynan. He drives through the South African desert to meet up with the next link and is surprised to find Mr. Wint and Mr. Kidd there waiting for him instead. They exchange formalities and Dr. Tynan gives them the diamonds. Then Kidd feigns pain from his wisdom teeth. As Tynan begins to examine Kidd, Wint walks behinds Tynan and drops the aforementioned scorpion down the doctor's shirt. The scorpion bites instantly and the dentist falls to the ground dead.

5. *Largo's solution for Quist in Thunderball*

SPECTRE henchman Quist (BILL CUMMINGS) arrives at villain Emilio Largo's (ADOLFO CELI) estate, Palmyra, from Bond's hotel room. He is sent to the pool area where Largo is waiting. "You saw Bond?" Largo asks. "Yes," answers Quist. "What happened?" asks Largo. Quist bows his head in shame and has no answer. Largo says to him disgustedly, "You let him get the better of you." He slaps Quist across the face and nods to his guards who seize Quist and hurl him into the pool which happens to be filled with Golden Grotto sharks.

The sharks attack and the pool rapidly turns red. One of the series' bloodier moments.

Honorable mention: Stromberg blowing Professor Markovitz and Dr. Bechman to bits in their helicopter in *The Spy Who Loved Me*; Milton Krest being depressurized and splattered by Sanchez in *Licence To Kill*.

Villain Deaths

Fortunately for mankind, many of the Bond villains who have been responsible for some imaginative deaths over the years, have suffered interesting deaths themselves. The five most memorable are:

1. Goldfinger in Goldfinger

While battling 007 (SEAN CONNERY) on board a private jet at the film's climax, the gun Goldfinger (GERT FROBE) is struggling with Bond for goes off, shooting out one of the jet's windows. The immediate cabin de-pressurization causes Goldfinger to be sucked out of the broken porthole and hurled into the atmosphere.

*Goldfinger (GERT FROBE) and Bond (SEAN CONNERY)
fight to the death in* Goldfinger

*As Bond (TIMOTHY DALTON) watches, Sanchez (ROBERT DAVI)
goes up in flames in* Licence to Kill

2. *Franz Sanchez in Licence To Kill*

Sanchez (ROBERT DAVI) and Bond (TIMOTHY DALTON) have just fallen off an oil tanker truck. Sanchez, doused in oil, makes his way over to 007, who is lying on the ground. As Sanchez raises a machete to apply the final blow to Bond, Bond takes out his lighter and flicks it; its extra-long flame ignites the oil-soaked Sanchez turning him into a human torch.

3. *Hugo Drax in Moonraker*

With his laser gun trained on an unarmed Bond (ROGER MOORE) Drax (MICHAEL LONSDALE) thinks he has 007 cornered onboard his space station. Drax is about to fire when 007 flicks his wrist, which activates a gadget that fires a poison dart into Drax's heart. As the dying Drax gasps for air, Bond leads him into an airlock. "Take a giant leap for mankind," Bond comments as he pushes the button that will catapult Drax into outer space.

Did you know that?

007 has killed Bond villains in some elaborate ways, but he has only shot three—Scaramanga in *The Man with the Golden Gun*, Stromberg in *The Spy Who Loved Me*, and Elektra in *The World Is Not Enough*.

4. *Elliot Carver in Tomorrow Never Dies*

James Bond (PIERCE BROSNAN) has finally gotten the better of media giant Elliot Carver (JONATHAN PRYCE). After battling each other on Carver's sinking stealth ship an exhausted Bond has an equally exhausted Carver in his grip. How should Bond administer the final blow? The answer is made for him: Carver's massive underwater drilling device, the Sea Drill, smashes into the room where they are. The huge drill spins toward them and Bond offers up Carver for the spinning teeth of the drill to dis-member.

5. *Kananga in Live and Let Die*

Bond (ROGER MOORE) and Kananga (YAPHET KOTTO) have fallen into a shark-laden canal inside Kananga's under-

Harold Sakata as Odd Job in Goldfinger

ground lair. As they battle it out underwater, Bond shoves a compressed-air shark pellet from his shark gun into Kananga's mouth. The pellet releases its air and inflates Kananga like a balloon, which causes him to shoot out of the water into the air, where he literally pops to pieces.

The Henchmen

Even the baddest of Bond villains needs a little help if he's going to hold the western powers to ransom or rule the world. He needs someone at his side who can wash the car, take out the garbage and, oh yes, kill people on command! It helps if this person is quite large, enormously strong and able to kill people in a fashion that he can uniquely call his own. Here are the five best henchmen in the series:

1. Harold Sakata as Odd Job in Goldfinger

Odd Job is the prototypical Bond movie henchman: strong, silent, seemingly indestructible. With his hulking, rock-solid body, fierce judo chops and deadly steel-rimmed bowler hat, you almost believe that there is no way Bond (SEAN CONNERY) will ever overcome him. When he does, it's one of the highlights of the entire series.

2. Robert Shaw as Red Grant in *From Russia With Love*

Red Grant is without a doubt the most realistic of all Bond henchmen and therefore the scariest. When he calmly and coldly explains to 007 (SEAN CONNERY) just how he is going to execute him it is a chilling moment. And their final battle together is one for the ages.

3. Richard Kiel as Jaws in *The Spy Who Loved Me*

Jaws's appearance in *The Spy Who Loved Me* is one of the film's highlights (as opposed to his subsequent appearance in *Moonraker*, which is an embarrassment). In a way he is the Odd Job of the 70s: strong and silent and, instead of a steel-rimmed bowler, with steel teeth. While he fails in his attempts to kill Bond (ROGER MOORE), check out what he does to that shark!

Did you know that?

Two henchmen have switched to the "side of good" and helped James Bond accomplish his mission: Jaws in *Moonraker* and May Day (a henchwoman) in *A View To A Kill*.

Bond (ROGER MOORE) battles Jaws (RICHARD KIEL) in The Spy Who Loved Me

4. Herve Villachaize as Nick Nack in *The Man with the Golden Gun*

Although Herve Villachaize's Nick Nack never seems to pose real danger to 007 (ROGER MOORE), his weird, shrewd and wily portrayal allows him to steal every scene he is in. Don't you almost feel sorry for him at the end of the film when he, with tears of hatred in his eyes, attempts to kill 007 as Bond is about to make love to Mary Goodnight?

5. Benicio Del Toro as Dario in *Licence To Kill*

Like most of the villains in *Licence To Kill*, Benicio Del Toro's Dario is such a great bad guy because he is frighteningly real. Watch the devilish grin he gives Bond (TIMOTHY

DALTON) at the bar when Pam Bouvier (CAREY LOWELL) thrusts her shotgun into Dario's crotch, or how he spits at Bond as 007 hangs on for dear life on the conveyor at the end of the film or the way he sneers at Pam and says, "You're dead," in the same scene. He uses his minimal screen time memorably, especially his sense of menace.

Honorable mention: Julius Harris as Tee Hee in *Live and Let Die*, Kabir Bedi as Gobinda in *Octopussy*, Andreas Wisniewski as Necros in *The Living Daylights*.

Henchmen Deaths

The main villains in a Bond movie aren't the only ones who have suffered unusual deaths. Their ever-faithful henchmen have died in some spectacular ways as well. The five best are:

1. Odd Job in Goldfinger

007 (SEAN CONNERY) has just flung Odd Job's (HAROLD SAKATA) steel-rimmed bowler hat at the indestructible henchman. The hat misses Odd Job and jams itself between two metal poles. As Odd Job calmly walks over to retrieve it, 007 notices a live cable lying on the floor near the metal bars.

He dives to the floor, grabs the cable and touches it to the metal bars, just as Odd Job grasps the steel rim of his bowler. He is electrocuted instantly and the once indestructible Odd Job is no more.

2. *Dario in Licence To Kill*

The menacing Dario (BENICIO DEL TORO) has Bond (TIMO-THY DALTON) hanging precariously over a cocaine-processing machine with its saw-blades spinning at his feet. 007's hands are tied together with wire and the wire is caught on a metal truss above the conveyor that leads to the processor. Standing on a walkway, Dario bends and slowly saws away at the wire. With the final cut, Bond's hands spring free and he grabs onto the edge of the conveyor with one hand, although his feet are being dragged closer to the blades. Now all Dario has to do is kick Bond's hand away and 007 will be chopped to pieces. But the arrival of Pam Bouvier (CAREY

Did you know that?

There has been only one time when James Bond has shown mercy to an evil henchman. At the end of *The Man with the Golden Gun*, instead of killing Nick Nack, Bond wraps him in a heavy-duty netting and ties him high up the mast of the sailing junk that he and Mary Goodnight are escaping in.

LOWELL) in the nick of time distracts him. She shoots Dario and he falls onto the conveyor, still alive. Bond raises his free hand and pulls Dario down. As he falls forward, he grabs Bond, but Bond kicks him away and Dario drops into the blades. Another of the series more gruesome deaths.

3. Hans in You Only Live Twice

007 (SEAN CONNERY) needs to get to the control room in Blofeld's hideaway so that he can destroy Blofeld's "Intruder Missile." To do so he must get past Blofeld's hulking hench-man, Hans (RONALD RICH), first. They fight furiously and Bond is able to steal the key from Hans that he will need to blow-up the missile. With the key, Bond runs for the control

*Bond (SEAN CONNERY) feeds Hans (RONALD RICH)
to the piranha in* You Only Live Twice

room chased by Hans. He tackles Bond on a footbridge, below which is a pool filled with man-eating piranhas. Hans pummels Bond and is about to land the punch that will send Bond into the pool, when Bond ducks and flips Hans into the water. The piranhas instantly converge on Hans and devour him in seconds. "Bon appetit," says Bond.

4. Necros in The Living Daylights

007 (TIMOTHY DALTON) and Necros (ANDREAS WISNIEWSKI) are hanging from netting that hangs from the back of a Soviet transport plane as it is flying. The netting holds sacks of opium that have slid out the open back of the plane. As they struggle to hang on to the netting and fight at the same time, 007 lands a punch to Necros' face that makes him fall. But somehow Necros grabs Bond's boot with both hands and hangs on. Bond takes his knife and slowly cuts away the boot-laces. When he cuts them through, the boot flies off his foot and Necros, still holding it, falls to his death. Bond later observes, "He got the boot."

5. Gobinda in Octopussy

Poor Gobinda (KABIR BEDI) finds himself in a similar situation to Necros. He is on top of a flying plane, fighting it out with Bond (ROGER MOORE). As he swings his knife at Bond, Bond slides backwards and grabs the plane's antenna. He arcs it back as far as it can go and then lets it go. The antenna springs forward and smacks Gobinda in the face, whereupon he loses his grip and falls to his death.

Claudine Auger as Domino in Thunderball

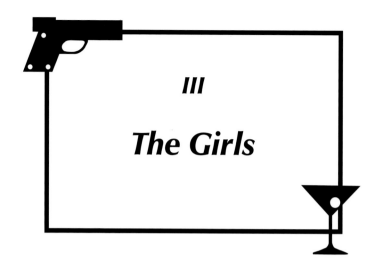

III

The Girls

In my opinion, the Bond girls have been given a bad rap. Sure they may be a bit more curvy and busty than your average woman, but where else will you find a group that includes a pilot, a diamond smuggler, a KGB agent, a tarot card reader, a NASA astronaut, a crossbow expert, a circus owner, a geologist, a cellist, a CIA helicopter pilot, and a nuclear physicist? Sounds like a group of intelligent, modern, independent women to me! Of course the actresses who have played these parts have never been confused with Meryl Streep and some have been better than others. Let's start with the "good" girls, the best and worst:

The Best "Good" Girls

1. Claudine Auger as Domino Vitale in Thunderball

As the young mistress of the villain Emilio Largo, Claudine Auger exhibits a human frailty and tenderness not seen in many Bond women. When she dances with Bond (SEAN CONNERY) outside the casino in Nassau, you feel her genuine need for Bond and Bond's sincere affection for her is clearly evident. Later in the film her pain is apparent when on the beach with Bond she learns the fate of her brother and accuses Bond of making love to her just to get to Largo. These two scenes are among the most realistic and heartfelt between Bond and a woman in the series and help make Domino stand out from the pack.

2. Diana Rigg as Tracy Di Vincenzo in On Her Majesty's Secret Service

It would need a strong, resourceful woman with a flair for living to bring James Bond to the altar and Diana Rigg as Tracy is just that kind of woman. She gambles, drives fast and wants the help of no one until she realizes that Bond (GEORGE LAZENBY) is the one who can save her from her reckless ways. She begins the film shaken and suicidal and ends it in love and at peace as 007's wife until a bullet takes that life in the most tragic Bond ending. A woman with a zest for life and adventure that makes it obvious why 007 falls so hard for her, and suffers so painfully when she is taken from him.

3. Barbara Bach as Anya Amasova in *The Spy Who Loved Me*

It took ten films for it to happen, but in *The Spy Who Loved Me*, James Bond (ROGER MOORE) finally meets his match in Anya Amasova, Agent XXX of the KGB. Amasova is the female James Bond, just as smart, tough and resourceful as 007. The two play a game of one-upmanship throughout the film, with Bond needing her help just as much as she needs his. The feminist movement finally reaches the world of James Bond!

Tracy (DIANA RIGG) embraces Bond (GEORGE LAZENBY) in On Her Majesty's Secret Service

4. Carey Lowell as Pam Bouvier in Licence To Kill

Like Anya Amasova before her, CIA agent Pam Bouvier is just as tough as Bond (TIMOTHY DALTON) and has no intention of playing second fiddle to him. When they arrive in Isthmus City pursuing drug lord Franz Sanchez, Bond explains to her, "we're south of the border. It's a man's world." She spends the rest of the film proving him wrong.

5. Carole Bouquet as Melina Havelock in For Your Eyes Only

Melina Havelock is not motivated by lust, greed or the need of Bond's protection. She simply wants revenge for the death of her parents and nothing, not the villains, not Bond,

Did you know that?

James Bond has been aided by a female agent of a foreign intelligence service six times: Kissy Suzuki of the Japanese Secret Service in *You Only Live Twice;* Rosie Carver of the CIA in *Live and Let Die;* Anya Amasova of the KGB in *The Spy Who Loved Me;* Holly Goodhead of the CIA in *Moonraker;* Pam Bouvier of the CIA in *Licence to Kill;* Wai Lin of the Chinese People's External Security Force in *Tomorrow Never Dies.*

will stand in her way. For this reason, Bond (ROGER MOORE) does not have her until the final scene—she's too consumed with exacting her revenge to waste time in bed. A three-dimensional woman with beauty and brains, she helps (not hinders, like some other Bond women) 007 complete his mission and save the day.

Honorable mention: Daniela Bianchi as Tatiana in *From Russia With Love*, Maud Adams as Octopussy in *Octopussy*, Isabella Scorupco as Natalya in *GoldenEye*.

The Worst "Good" Girls

1. Tanya Roberts as Stacy Sutton in *A View To A Kill*

It's easier for me to believe in Santa Claus than that Tanya Roberts is an expert geologist in *A View To A Kill*. Her throaty cries of "James!" and her annoyingly raspy screams are painful to listen to, and yet, they're better than watching her drive a firetruck or jump around the Golden Gate Bridge. Roberts' inept acting and bleach-blond Barbie looks help make *A View To A Kill* the major disappointment it is.

2. *Britt Ekland as Mary Goodnight in The Man with the Golden Gun*

When Mary Goodnight's bikini-clad tush accidently pushes the button that activates Scaramanga's solar panel, almost frying James Bond (ROGER MOORE) in the process, it really hits home that she has been much more of a danger to Bond in this film than any of the villains. Earlier when she gets locked in the trunk of Scaramanga's car, you kind of hope that she will stay there for the rest of the film. Worst of all she doesn't even look good in that ugly 70s bikini that she runs around in on Scaramanga's island,. It's one thing for a Bond girl to be a bad actress, but she should at least look good in a bikini!

3. *Maryam D'Abo as Kara Milovy in The Living Daylights*

The Living Daylights, released during the safe-sex trend of 1987 is the first (and only) Bond film to feature a "one woman" 007. Therefore it would have been nice if the one woman was up to snuff. She's not. It's not just that Maryam D'Abo isn't much of a looker compared to other Bond girls, it's that she is a whiny and helpless character. After seeing able Bond women as Barbara Bach, Carole Bouquet, and Maud Adams in recent Bond films, D'Abo's Kara Milovy makes you wish that she would just leave Bond (TIMOTHY DALTON) alone to get on with his mission! The film ends with has Bond saying to Kara, "You didn't think I'd miss this performance?" Well, James, I kind of wish that we all had.

Kara (MARYAM D'ABO) and Bond (TIMOTHY DALTON) in The Living Daylights

4. Lois Chiles as Dr. Holly Goodhead in Moonraker

It's hard to tell if Lois Chiles' performance as Holly Goodhead is a result of bad writing or bad acting. It's probably a little of both. To say that she's not exactly convincing as a CIA agent/NASA scientist is a slight understatement. Plus, her character comes across as annoying, to the point that you wonder why Bond (ROGER MOORE) would want anything to do with her, buxom looks aside.

5. *Talisa Soto as Lupe in Licence To Kill*

Soto's performance is the only one in the film that isn't top quality. Bottom line, she can't act. It's almost as if she's struggling to remember her lines as she says them. Fortunately, she looks pretty good, so you can understand why villain Franz Sanchez is so attached to her. And her screen time is slight enough as not to negatively affect the rest of the film.

Femmes Fatales

While virtually every woman in a Bond film wants to bed 007, some women want to bed him *and* kill him. And they seem to want both with equal passion. If only James had sent flowers the next day...

Here are the five best *femmes fatales*:

1. *Sophie Marceau as Elektra King in The World Is Not Enough*

It would be hard to underestimate the effectiveness of Sophie Marceau as Elektra King in *The World Is Not Enough*. Her chameleon-like performance, though hard to categorize, is the main reason the film is as good as it is. Elektra King is at the same time main villain and a *femme fatale*. Because of the hold she has on 007 (PIERCE BROSNAN) and because of the way she manipulates and toys with his head as well as his emotions is why I've chosen her as a *femme fatale*. We first see Elektra as a helpless victim who Bond must protect. But gradually we come to realize that Elektra has been playing Bond (and everyone else) for fools. When Bond first begins to suspect her of villainy, he is so enamored with her that he allows her to talk her way out of it. His misstep brings dire consequences for everyone involved. We've never seen a

Elektra (SOPHIE MARCEAU) straddles 007 (PIERCE BROSNAN) in The World Is Not Enough

Did you know that?

Although the series has had many *femme fatales*, Bond has been intimate with only 3 of them: Fiona in *Thunderball*, May Day in *A View To A Kill*, and Elektra in *The World Is Not Enough*.

woman before who can make Bond doubt his own instincts. Even in their final confrontation, Bond gives Elektra every chance to save herself. Of course, after pulling him on a string for most of the film, Elektra is convinced that Bond won't hurt her. "You wouldn't kill me, James," she says seductively as Bond points a gun at her, "You'd miss me." But Bond proves her wrong by coldly pulling the trigger and killing her. "I never miss," he states.

2. *Luciana Paluzzi as Fiona Volpe in Thunderball*

A line in *Thunderball* clearly illustrates why Luciana Paluzzi is one of the best *femmes fatales* of the series. She and Bond (SEAN CONNERY) have just had "wild" sex as Bond terms it, but Volpe's henchmen show up immediately afterwards to capture Bond. Bond informs her that he knew she was working for the bad guys all along and adds, "what I did tonight was for king and country. Don't think it gave me any pleasure." To which she replies, "James Bond. Who only has to make love to a woman once before she hears choir bells and immediately turns to the side of good and virtue. But not this one!" She is fiery, sexy and ruthless and relishes her opportunity to kill Bond, which of course she fails to do. But we have a great time watching her try!

3. Lotte Lenya as Rosa Klebb in *From Russia With Love*

Lotte Lenya's Rosa Klebb may not be considered by some as a *femme fatale*; there's a lot of "fatale" and not so much "femme." But she is certainly a deadly and dangerous foe for 007 (SEAN CONNERY). Plotting and planning the murder and humiliation of Bond, takes her through the entire film although they don't actually meet until the movie's final minutes. But what a memorable meeting that is: Klebb surprises Bond in his hotel room and attempts to stab him to death by kicks with a poison-tipped dagger that springs from the front of her shoe! Not the kind of woman you want to be alone with in a room!

4. Famke Janssen as Xenia Onatopp in *GoldenEye*

From her name alone you know that Xenia is going to be a handful for Bond (PIERCE BROSNAN). Only a Bond film would have a woman who kills people by strangling them with her thighs! She not only likes to kill people in this manner, but she also screeches in orgasmic delight whenever she does.

She encounters Bond in a steam room and yes she wants to kill him, but not until she wraps her legs around him and climaxes first! If 007 were ever going to die, I'm sure he would have chosen this moment to do it!

5. Caroline Munro as Naomi in *The Spy Who Loved Me*

Naomi (CAROLINE MUNRO), Karl Stromberg's assassin doesn't have a large speaking role, but when you look like she does, you don't need one! Despite all the sexy, lustful looks she trades with Bond, they unfortunately never come together. The closest they come is when Bond (ROGER MOORE) fires a rocket at Naomi's helicopter that sends her to a fiery death, then you sense that Bond would rather have given her a different projectile!

Bond (PIERCE BROSNAN) confronts Xenia (FAMKE JANSSEN) in GoldenEye

Sexiest Moments

For all of their sexual innuendo, the James Bond films have consistently been rated PG (or PG-13) and considered suitable for the whole family. Generally, the sexual inferences are such that they go right over the head of your average 10-year-old. And all of the sex scenes fade out after the first kiss. But this doesn't mean that these scenes don't generate some heat. They do. The five hottest scenes are:

1. Thunderball

This movie probably has the most overt sexual tone in the series. The scene which opens with Bond (SEAN CONNERY) returning to his hotel room in the Bahamas and being surprised when he hears splashing coming from his bathroom, shows how. When he opens the bathroom door to investigate, he finds the voluptuous Fiona Volpe (LUCIANA PAOLUZZI) sitting in the tub wearing nothing but a towel wrapped around her hair. "Oh!" a supposedly surprised Fiona exclaims when she sees Bond peering at her. "Hello," replies an obviously turned-on 007. "Aren't you in the wrong room, Mr. Bond?" she asks. "Not from where I'm standing," Bond says devilishly as he continues to enjoy the view. "Since you are here, would you mind giving me something to put on?" she asks. Bond picks up Fiona's slippers, walks over to the tub and hands them to her. Then he sits in a chair, casually crosses his legs, and waits for Fiona to get out of the bath. Disconcerted that Bond has only given her a pair of slippers to wear, Fiona unwraps the towel from her hair and stands up slowly, using the scrap of towel to barely shield her

Fiona (LUCIANA PALUZZI) undresses Bond (SEAN CONNERY) in Thunderball

body. Bond sits back and enjoys the show as she dries off. "Anyway, I'm very glad to see you again, Mr. Bond," she comments. Continuing to eye her up, Bond responds, "I'm glad to see you again." Fiona steps out of the tub as their conversation continues. Both feign surprise that they were "mistakenly" put in the same hotel room. Moving towards Bond finally, Fiona asks, "Shouldn't you get out of these wet clothes?" as she aggressively pulls Bond's shirt over his head. The scene fades out.

2. From Russia With Love

Another hotel room. Another treat waiting. This time James is in Instanbul. Returning to his room, Bond (SEAN CONNERY) goes to his bathroom to draw a bath. He hears noises coming from the bedroom (Bond happens to be staying in the honeymoon suite!) as he undresses. Bond wraps a towel around his waist, grabs his gun and walks into the bedroom just in time to see a nude woman slip into his bed and wrap herself in the sheets. Gun in hand, Bond approaches the bed. The woman says, "You look surprised. I thought you were expecting me." Bond realizes that this is the Russian cipher clerk (DANIELA BIANCHI) who he has been sent to "contact." "So you're Tatiana Romanova," he says. "My friends call me Tania," she says. "Mine call me James Bond," he replies. As Bond stands beside the bed, they shake hands. "Well, now that we've been properly introduced . . . ," Bond says as he moves in to kiss her. But Tania stops him, saying, "Guns upset me." "I'm sorry. I'm a bit . . . upset myself," Bond comments. "You look just like your, your photograph," Tania says lustily. "You're one of the

most beautiful girls I've ever seen," says Bond. "Thank you.
But I think my mouth is too big," she says. "No, it's the right
size," Bond says as the camera does a close-up of Tania licking
her lips. "For me that is," he adds as he bends down and
plants a rather aggressive kiss on them. Business intervenes.
Bond and Tania discuss how she will steal a Soviet encoding
machine for him. But, business talk over, they get back to
more pressing matters. Tania embraces Bond and slides her
hands down his back to finger a scar. "You see, I know all
about you from your file," she tells him. "You do? Well I hope
you're not disappointed," he replies. "I will tell you in the
morning," she responds as Bond climbs on top of her.

3. Thunderball

Patricia Fearing (MOLLY PETERS), an employee at the Shrub-
lands Health Spa outside of London where James Bond (SEAN
CONNERY) is staying, has just taken some x-rays of him which
the two are reviewing. "Do I seem healthy?" Bond asks. "Too
healthy, by far," she replies. Without provocation, Bond
drops his arms around her and starts kissing her. She struggles, trying to fend him off and does eventually break Bond's
grip on her. "Behave yourself Mr. Bond! Oh, I can see there's
only one place to keep you quiet," she exclaims. Whereupon
she takes him to another room that contains a spine-
stretching mechanism called "the rack." She efficiently
straps Bond in and leaves the room. The villainous Count
Lippe sneaks into the room after she exits and messes with
the "rack's" controls, causing the mechanism to speed up so
much that it almost stretches Bond beyond endurance. Luck-

Did you know that?

James Bond has been intimate with many women over the course of 19 films—the four he enjoyed in *A View To A Kill* being a one-film record: the submarine-driver in the pretitle sequence, May Day, Pola Ivanova, and Stacy Sutton.

ily for 007, Patricia happens back and switches the machine off before it can do more harm. Bond climbs off of the contraption and the two leave the room. As they walk by the steam room, Bond says, "Somebody's going to wish today had never happened." "Oh, you wouldn't tell Dr. Wayne," Patricia cries. "Please, I'd lose my job," she begs. Sensing an opportunity, Bond's mood brightens and he hints, "Well I suppose my silence could have a price." "You don't mean?!!" she asks. Bond smiles rakishly. "Oh no" she says as she wags her finger at him. But Bond draws her hastily into the steam room. "Oh yes" he says as he disrobes Patricia. As the scene fades out, we see her bare skin press up against the glass of the room.

4. GoldenEye

In an indoor pool at the Grand Hotel Europe in St. Petersburg, Russia, James Bond (PIERCE BROSNAN) is swimming alone. As he floats, he notices out of the corner of his eye a figure sneak into the steam room adjoining the pool. Sensing danger, Bond climbs out of the pool, takes his gun, and heads for the steam room. He enters and seizes the arm of the person, who he flings into the center of the room. Bond sees it is the villainous Xenia Onattop (FAMKE JANSSEN) who works for the Janus Crime Syndicate, the group he has been searching for. Bond points his gun at her. He wonders if she's here for pleasure or pain. "You don't need the gun, Commander," she suggests. "That depends on your definition of safe sex," Bond replies. Xenia smiles and steps towards Bond. "That's close enough," he says. "Not for what I have in mind," she says as she grabs him and starts kissing him. Bond drops his gun and the two go at it vigorously. Xenia actually starts to become orgasmic (her specialty) and bites Bond's lip, drawing blood. They break apart. Now Bond is confused; what is going on? Before he can figure it out, Xenia is "on-a-top" of him, squeezing the life from him with her vise like thighs (her other specialty). Bond tries desperately to escape her hold. He slams Xenia into the wall. Nothing works. He can't break free. The harder he tries, the more orgasmic she gets! At last Bond is able to flip her onto the hot steam which looses her grip on him. He is then confronted by one of Xenia's thugs who enters the room; but Bond ably knocks him out. Xenia takes another lunge at him and he uses her momentum to flip her over his head and onto the floor. Bond regains his gun and points it at the defeated Onattop. "No, no, no, no more foreplay. Take me to Janus," he commands. Not exactly Bond's most romantic encounter, but definitely sexy.

5. *Goldfinger*

While the sexual overtones of the following scene from *Goldfinger* are a little more subtle than the four previous scenes, the sexual prowess of Bond (SEAN CONNERY) combined with the erotic mannerisms of Jill Masterson (SHIRLEY EATON) still make for a pretty hot scene. It begins with Bond furtively entering Goldfinger's hotel suite (by now it should be obvious that Bond has plenty of nice encounters in hotels) and finding the delicate Jill lying on the balcony wearing very skimpy, very sexy black underwear. She is using a telescope and a radio to help Goldfinger cheat at his gin game, which is taking place at poolside below the balcony. Bond walks onto the balcony and turns off the radio. Startled, Jill jumps up and says "Who are you?!" as 007 replies as confident as ever, "Bond...James Bond." Bond peers through the telescope to witness Goldfinger's cheating in action and Jill calms somewhat. She is taken with this good-looking stranger named James Bond. "What's your name?" Bond asks. "Jill," she replies. "Jill who?" he continues. "Jill Masterson," she tells him. "Tell me, Jill," Bond says, "why does he do it?" "He likes to win," she says. "Why do you do it?" he asks. "He pays me," she replies. "Is that all he pays you for?" Bond goes on. "And for being seen with him," she adds. "Just seen?" Bond asks. "Just seen," she emphasizes. "I'm so glad," Bond responds as he gazes at the scantily clad Jill. "You're much too nice to be mixed up in anything like this you know," he adds. 007 turns the radio back on and orders Goldfinger to lose $15,000 at his gin game or he, Bond, will turn him over to the Miami Beach Police. Bond's audacity at dealing with Goldfinger quite impresses Jill and she says, "I'm beginning to like you, Mr. Bond ." "No, call me James," he says. "More that anyone I've met in a long time, James," she adds. "Well, what on earth are we going to do about it?" Bond asks seductively. "Yes, what?" Jill echoes. "I'll tell you at dinner," Bond says as he moves closer to her. "Where?" a very turned-on Jill asks. "Well, I know the best place in town...," Bond answers as he kisses the ready, willing and able Ms. Masterson.

Fashion

Although getting women out of their clothes has been a "career" for James Bond, in many cases it is the alluring attire they wear (or almost wear) that has led to their undressing. The 5 girl outfits that are the five sexiest are:

1. The White Bikini worn by Honey Ryder in Dr. No

The white bikini-clad Ursula Andress standing in the shallow water of Crab Key beach has to be one of the most enduring in not only Bond—but film—history. It's not the bikini itself as much as the tanned, voluptuous body that it covers (barely!). And with a knife, strapped to the bikini bottom, which Honey whips out in a show of force to Bond, 007 (SEAN CONNERY), and the audience, know that this Bond girl is more than a pretty body in a sexy bikini.

Honey (URSULA ANDRESS) makes a memorable entrance in Dr. No

Did you know that?

Only five lead Bond girls have appeared in a bikini: Ursula Andress as Honey in *Dr. No;* Claudine Auger as Domino in *Thunderball;* Mie Hama as Kissy in *You Only Live Twice;* Jill St. John as Tiffany in *Diamonds Are Forever;* Britt Ekland as Mary in *The Man with the Golden Gun.*

2. The Ice-skating outfit that Tracy di Vincenzo wears in On Her Majesty's Secret Service

James Bond (GEORGE LAZENBY) has just escaped from Blofeld's mountain lair, Piz Gloria. Unarmed and in serious danger because Blofeld's thugs are pursuing him, he threads his way through the local village below. He spots a crowded outdoor skating rink and decides to sit at the rinkside and watch skaters, thereby hoping to blend in with the crowd. He lowers his head and draws his coat collar up around his face, when he notices two ice skates attached to two very sexy legs skate right up to him. Bond looks up and sees Tracy (DIANA RIGG), his soon-to-be wife, standing before him in the sexiest skating outfit that he (or I) has ever seen. The outfit's short miniskirt barely covers Tracy's nether regions and does a fantastic job of showing off her scrumptious thighs. I am almost convinced that it is the irresistible sight of Tracy in this outfit that made James Bond fall in love with her.

3. The Indian Sari that wraps Magda in Octopussy

Magda (KRISTINA WAYBORN) wears a glamorous sari as she and Bond (ROGER MOORE) eat dinner in India. They retire to Bond's hotel room and we see what makes it special. After a round of love-making, and thinking that Bond is asleep, Magda slips out of bed. She wraps herself in her sari and

Bond (ROGER MOORE) and Magda (KRISTINA WAYBORN) in Octopussy

steals 007's Faberge egg, which she hides (and which Bond is letting her steal) in the loosely draped top of the sari. Bond awakens, so she retreats to the balcony and rapidly ties one end of the sari to the parapet, before turning to face Bond, who is up and walking towards her. "I don't know how to say goodbye," she says. "Actions speak louder than words," Bond says and he bends over to kiss her. But Magda leans back and rolls over the edge of the balcony, from which she descends quickly. The sari unravels as she goes, until it is completely off her and Magda reaches the ground, clad only in bra and panties. The sari, still attached to the balcony, blows in the wind. Villain Kamal Khan's car pulls up beside her and Magda is whisked away. This is the only time that a seductive outfit (or any outfit) has been used as a means of escape. But at least Bond got to enjoy the sight of Magda removing herself from it!

4. Paris Carver's undergarments in Tomorrow Never Dies

Paris Carver (TERI HATCHER) shows up at Bond's hotel suite in Hamburg, dressed in a quite magnificent and voluptuous black evening dress. Even more magnificent is what is under this dress. Bond (PIERCE BROSNAN) and Paris kiss and he slowly removes her dress to reveal the hottest set of black panties, garter belt and stockings ever seen in the series. Of course, it helps that these garments are on the body of Teri Hatcher, and that they kiss so passionately. Unfortunately the scene fades out at this point (remember, this is a Bond movie) before we find out what is under those garments.

5. The Naval uniform that outfits Anya Amasova in The Spy Who Loved Me

It is said that there is nothing like a man in uniform. Well, the same can be said about a woman in uniform—especially if the woman is Major Anya Amasova (BARBARA BACH) of the KGB. When Bond (ROGER MOORE) and Anya join the crew of an American submarine in search of villain Karl Stromberg's oil tanker, they both don appropriate naval dress. Anya's flowing hair, soft skin and runway-model face make such a contrast with the conservative uniform, that it is difficult to notice Bond or anyone else in the scene.

Bond Girl Names

It wouldn't seem right for super-stud James Bond to go out with or be associated with any plain Jane, Jill or Nancy. No, to go out with someone as worldly as 007, a man who is lusted after by women around the globe, a woman had better have a more creative name than Jane! Here are the five best Bond-girl names:

Xenia Onatopp (FAMKE JANSSEN) takes aim in GoldenEye

1. Pussy Galore in Goldfinger

A strange blond woman is staring 007 (SEAN CONNERY) in the face when he awakes on Goldfinger's private jet after being drugged. "My name is Pussy," she says, "Pussy Galore." "I must be dreaming," a sluggish Bond replies. Yes, Pussy Galore (HONOR BLACKMAN), the name that started the tradition and a name that some would say captures the essence of what James Bond films are all about.

2. Holly Goodhead in Moonraker

Does Holly Goodhead (LOIS CHILES) live up to her suggestive moniker? Being that Bond movies are family films, we never find out. But since Roger Moore has a smile on his face for most of this film, we'll assume that she does.

3. Chiu Mi in The Man with the Golden Gun

We only see Chiu Mi briefly as she skinny-dips in the pool of evil industrialist Hai Fat (another good name, but it doesn't fit the category) and she does nothing particularly noteworthy, but when she introduces herself as Chiu Mi, how can we forget her?

4. Xenia Onatopp in GoldenEye

Since Xenia Onatopp (FAMKE JANSSEN) kills men by crushing them with her thighs, she's one woman you'd rather not have "on-a-top" of you. Of course 007 (PIERCE BROSNAN) fails to avoid this situation, but comes out on top in the end.

5. Plenty O'Toole in Diamonds Are Forever

When Plenty O'Toole (LANA WOOD) sidles up to Bond (SEAN CONNERY) at the craps table where he's playing in a Vegas casino and says cheerfully to him, "Hi, I'm Plenty." Bond glances at her attributes and replies, "But of course you are." "Plenty O'Toole," she clarifies. "Named after your father, perhaps?" Bond responds.

Sean Connery as James Bond

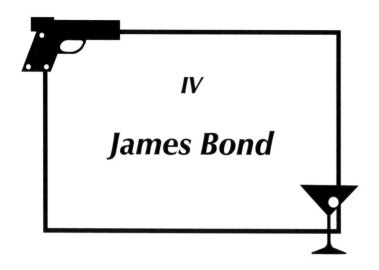

IV

James Bond

James Bond. The man who every male wants to be, and every female wants to be with. The man who is the smoothest, most debonair character there is. The man who has all the best cars, gets all the best women, and uses all of the coolest gadgets. The man who out-wits the most diabolical bad guys and saves the world about every two years. And the man who looks good and keeps his sense of humor through it all. And he hasn't aged a day in 40 years!

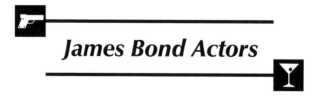

James Bond Actors

For most people, their favorite Bond actor is the one they saw first as Bond. I am fortunate to have seen the Bonds (with the exception of Lazenby) in order of their appearance. When all is said and done, I like all five of the actors who have played Bond; it is the unique touches they each have brought to the role that have helped keep the series fresh for 40 years. But I do have a pecking order, which is:

1. Sean Connery

Sean Connery is quite simply the ultimate cinematic version of James Bond and the one his successors will always be compared to unfavorably. In fact, his portrayal of 007 created the antihero—the guy who can be just as nasty, ruthless, and cold as the bad guys he is chasing. Connery's Bond also was the first of the witty action heroes, the guy who always has a funny throwaway line to keep the mood light after a tense situation (a trait copied two decades later by the likes of Arnold Schwarzenegger and Bruce Willis). He maintains Bond's tough, macho, chauvinistic, supremely confident and always cool image without ever losing his suave demeanor and

Did you know that?

The following actors were seriously considered for the role of James Bond: Richard Burton in *Dr. No*; Burt Reynolds in *Diamonds Are Forever*; James Brolin in *Octopussy*; Sam Neill in *The Living Daylights*; Ralph Fiennes in *GoldenEye*.

Pierce Brosnan

charm. He could kiss you, kill you, and order a bottle of champagne within the same minute and not think twice about it. Although this interpretation of the character is different from Ian Fleming's literary creation (who was a more human character with frailties, fears, imperfections, and no humor), it was the perfect persona for the style of the films. When Connery says his name is "Bond, James Bond," you believe it!

2. Pierce Brosnan

Pierce Brosnan is the only actor in the Bond role, other than Connery, able to combine toughness, sexuality, charm and humor, and this ability earns him his number two spot on the list. Roger Moore has great charm and humor, Timothy Dalton was great at being tough and serious, but it is Brosnan who is able to display all of these characteristics and that makes him the closest thing to Connery that we have seen. Brosnan's Bond is also much more believable as a chauvinistic babe magnet than the aging Moore or the soft-spoken Dalton. Whether he's engaged in humorous banter with Moneypenny in *GoldenEye,* killing in cold blood in *Tomorrow Never Dies,* or seducing Dr. Warmflash in *The World Is Not Enough,* Bond by Brosnan is a Bond to be reckoned with.

Roger Moore

3. Roger Moore

When Roger Moore appeared first as James Bond in 1973, it marked a significant change in the cinematic nature of the character. Gone were the macho toughness and ruthlessness of Connery's Bond. In their place, Moore played up Bond's suave and humorous side and his films reflected this new tone. Moore's Bond was more of an international playboy than a man licenced to kill, and who seemed more comfortable with a wisecrack than cracking someone in the face with his fist. Still, Moore always comes across as confident and assured and his lighter take on the role is entertaining to watch. In some of his later films, especially *For Your Eyes Only* and *Octopussy*, Moore actually does play a more serious Bond and pulls it off surprisingly well, although his aging face and expanding waistline in these films do not work as well. Moore must be given credit for keeping the series alive after Connery's departure and for proving that audiences could accept someone else in the role.

4. Timothy Dalton

Because he appeared in only two Bond films, it is hard to judge Timothy Dalton fairly as 007. Connery, Moore, and Brosnan were able to develop and improve their portrayals over several films. Not afforded the same chance, Dalton's short tenure in the role must be judged incomplete. He attempted to distinguish himself from Connery and Moore by going back to Ian Fleming's characterization of Bond and portraying a realistic, human 007. Gone were Con-

Timothy Dalton

nery's machismo and Moore's charm and humor. Dalton's serious approach was a departure for the series and a fresh and welcome sea-change after 12 years of Moore's light-comedic style. In the end, this portrayal was almost too serious. The cinematic Bond must be suave and charming and have at least *some* humor. Without these qualities Dalton's brooding Bond, while an interesting and noble departure from the norm, misses the mark. Had he been given more films to do, his Bond may have developed into a more complete character.

5. George Lazenby

George Lazenby must be given credit for the fact that as a man with no prior acting experience, his performance is not an embarrassment and the film in which he appears, *On Her Majesty's Secret Service,* is one of the very best of the series. For the filmgoer, Lazenby's lack of acting experience is painfully evident early in the film, especially during some extended dialogue scenes. As the film progresses, though, and the action picks up, Lazenby seems more comfortable and by the end of the film you can accept that he is James Bond. But, as with Dalton, we'll never know how successful he could have been in future films.

George Lazenby

007 (SEAN CONNERY) kills in cold blood in Dr. No

Cold Blooded Killings

For all that James Bond can be funny, lighthearted and amusing, he can sometimes be a ruthless killer. And this is when true Bond fans like him best. The five killings with 007 at his chilling best are in:

1. Dr. No

Bond (SEAN CONNERY) sits in Miss Taro's room in a chair, waiting for Dr. No henchman, Professor Dent (ANTHONY

DAWSON), who he knows is coming to kill him. Bond has padded the bed with pillows to make it look as if he is in it asleep. The ruse works. Dent sneaks in the room and empties his pistol into the pillows. Then 007 flicks on the light and holds his silenced Walther PPK on Dent. Dent drops his gun and sits down as Bond questions him. The questions go on, until Dent dives to the floor, grabs his gun and fires at Bond, but no bullets come out—he already emptied his gun into the bed! Bond, of course, knew this all along, and says to him, "That's a Smith & Wesson. And you've had your six." He then coldly pumps a bullet into Dent. When Dent's body hits the floor, Bond pumps another bullet into him for good measure before he icily removes his silencer and slowly blows away the smoke emanating from it. This scene represents Bond (and Connery) at his ruthless best.

2. *The World Is Not Enough*

In *The World Is Not Enough,* James Bond (PIERCE BROSNAN) has had a rough go at it. He feels guilty at having failed to protect the life of Elektra King's father, Sir Robert. Then, while protecting Elektra (SOPHIE MARCEAU), he reluctantly falls in love with her. But, he begins to doubt her loyalties. Unfortunately he fails to act in time to keep her from proceeding with her evil plans, for when he finally realizes that she is the villain he has been searching for all along, her henchmen have captured him and brought him to her. She promptly ties him down in an ancient Turkish torture chair and is seconds from killing him when Bond frees himself (with the help of old friend Valentin Zukovsky). After a brief struggle, Elektra gets away and runs up the spiral staircase of her Maiden's Tower. Halfway up, she pauses, looks down at the pursuing Bond, and taunts him, "You can't kill me James. Not in cold blood!" Bond, more determined than ever, races up after her. During the climb he hears the kidnapped M scream, "Bond!" He turns and sees M locked in a cell. He hastily fires at the lock and continues up the stairs. When reaches the top he finds Elektra waiting for him, confident that Bond won't harm her. Bond hands her a walkietalkie and orders her to call off Renard, her partner in crime who waits outside and below in a submarine that will soon destroy Istanbul. "Call him off," Bond tersely tells her. She smiles at him seductively. "I won't ask you again, Elektra," he says. "Call him off!" he shouts. She replies in her sweetest voice, "You wouldn't kill me, James. You'd miss me." She then screams into the walkie-talkie to Renard, "Dive, Dive"— but she is cut off as Bond's gun cuts her down. Staring at her fallen body, he says grimly, "I never miss."

3. Tomorrow Never Dies

The sinister Dr. Kaufman (VINCENT SCHIAVELLI) has murdered Bond's old flame, Paris (TERI HATCHER), and is on the verge of shooting Bond when Stamper interrupts him by radio to say they can't get into Bond's car to retrieve the GPS satellite encoder that Bond has stolen from Carver's lab. Stamper orders Kaufman to make Bond tell him how to get in the car. Kaufman says he is to torture 007 if he won't do so. Bond calmly explains that his cell phone opens the car and takes the phone out of his jacket pocket. Kaufman stiffens and says, "No, no, Mr. Bond. I do it." Bond hands him the phone slowly and tells him, "Recall, three, send..." Kaufman follows Bond's instructions and the phone zaps him with an electric shock, which allows 007 to jump up and snatch for Kaufman's gun. They struggle for it until Bond wrests it from Kaufman and turns the weapon to within an inch of Kaufman's face. "I'm just a professional doing a job," pleads Kaufman. "Me too," replies Bond as he pulls the trigger.

4. For Your Eyes Only

The murderous Emil Locque (MICHAEL GOTHARD), who has killed Bond ally Luigi Ferrara of the Italian Secret Service, is speeding away in his car along a mountain road in Albania.

Did you know that?

James Bond has used a knife to kill or injure an opponent in seven films: *Dr. No* (Dr. No's guard in the pond on Crab Key); *From Russia With Love* (Red Grant); *Thunderball* (Largo's henchman in the pool at Palmyra); *You Only Live Twice* (Henderson's assassin); *Diamonds Are Forever* (Blofeld's guards in the pretitle sequence); *Octopussy* (Grischka); *Tomorrow Never Dies* (Carver's guard outside of the stealth ship).

But due to the winding nature of the road, Bond (ROGER MOORE) catches up with him on foot and fires several shots at Locque's car that send it off the road, where it teeters on the edge of a cliff. Locque is wounded and struggles to keep balanced as the car hangs precariously. Bond walks over to the car slowly and drops a small pin of a white dove onto Locque's lap, the same pin that Locque left on the dead Ferrara's lap. "You left this with Ferrara, I believe," says Bond. With a vicious kick at the side of the car, he sends it and Locque over the edge.

5. Licence To Kill

Federal Agent Ed Killifer has betrayed 007's best friend, Felix Leiter, by helping drug lord Franz Sanchez, whom Bond and Leiter have captured, to escape. Sanchez subsequently has Leiter's new wife murdered and he feeds Leiter to the sharks (he survives). About to leave town with a suitcase filled with the 2 million dollars he was paid for his assistance Killifer runs into Bond at Milton Krest's sea-life warehouse. He pulls a gun on Bond (TIMOTHY DALTON) and opens a trap-door in the floor to a cage that holds a couple of man-eating sharks, the same sharks that maimed Felix Leiter. On the verge of forcing Bond to join the sharks, Killifer is knocked off balance by Bond's friend and ally, Sharkey, who thrusts up from another trapdoor in the floor. Because he is knocked off balance, Killifer drops his suitcase, grabs onto a cable that hangs from the ceiling above the sharks and hangs on precariously. Bond picks up the cash-filled suitcase and Killifer yells, "There's 2 million dollars in that case. I'll split it with you." Bond replies, "You earnt it, you keep it old buddy" and hurls the case at Killifer, which knocks him from the cable into the jaws of the waiting sharks.

One-Liners

James Bond's unflappability is due in part to his use of humor to lighten the mood in a tense situation. If he ever loses his license to kill, he just might have a future doing stand-up in Vegas. My choice of his five funniest one-liners is:

1. Thunderball

Bond (SEAN CONNERY) has just escaped from SPECTRE assassin Fiona Volpe (LUCIANA PALUZZI) and is racing through the local Junkanoo Festival while Volpe and her henchmen search desperately for him. To blend in at an outside dance club Bond grabs an unsuspecting beauty and leads her onto the dance floor. Just as the dance begins, another woman—Volpe!—cuts in on the beauty. As Volpe and Bond dance, he scans the club rapidly for Volpe's henchmen. The music gets louder, just as Bond spots a pistol protruding from behind the band and directed right at him. At the point of discharge, Bond swirls Volpe around and the bullet intended for him hits her in the back, killing her instantly. Bond supports her body and casually slides her over to a nearby table, where he gently places her upright in a chair and deadpans to a couple of perplexed patrons, "Do you mind if my friend sits this one out? She's just dead."

2. Thunderball

Bond (SEAN CONNERY) and Domino (CLAUDINE AUGER) are sitting on the beach, when Domino notices SPECTRE assassin Vargas (PHILIP LOCKE) with silenced pistol in hand sneaking up behind them. She tells Bond, "Vargas, behind you." "Really?" Bond replies as he nonchalantly picks up his underwater spear gun and fires. The spear passes through Vargas and impales him on a tree. "I think he got the point," quips Bond.

Did you know that?

While undercover James Bond has used the following aliases: David Somerset (*From Russia With Love*); Mr. Fisher (*You Only Live Twice*); Sir Hilary Bray (*On Her Majesty's Secret Service*); Peter Franks and Klaus Hergescheimer (*Diamonds Are Forever*); Francisco Scaramanga (*The Man with the Golden Gun*); Robert Sterling (*The Spy Who Loved Me*); James St. John-Smythe and James Stock (*A View To A Kill*).

Did you know that?

The line "Bond. James Bond." is one of the most recognizable lines of dialogue in film history. Yet, as much of a staple of the Bond formula as that line is, there are three films where Bond does not say it: *From Russia With Love*; *Thunderball*; and *You Only Live Twice*.

3. Goldfinger

Bond (SEAN CONNERY) first hurls a Mexican assassin into a tub full of water, then follows him with a plugged-in heater. The assassin is electrocuted. Exiting the room, Bond looks back and says, "Shocking. Positively shocking."

4. Diamonds Are Forever

Bond (SEAN CONNERY) has just brought Plenty O'Toole (LANA WOOD) back to his darkened Las Vegas hotel room. They begin to kiss passionately and Bond is starting to remove her clothes, when she excuses herself to the bathroom. Bond comes fully into the room and turns on the lights, only to find three thugs pointing guns at him. "I'm afraid you've caught me with more than my hands up," says Bond.

Bond (ROGER MOORE) holds his piece in
The Man with the Golden Gun

5. *The Man with the Golden Gun*

Bond (ROGER MOORE) is trying to get the gunsmith (MARNE MAITLAND) who makes the special gold bullets for Francisco Scaramanga to tell him how and where he delivers the bullets to Scaramanga. But the gunmaker won't easily give up the information. So Bond moves the rifle he has been holding on the man to point at the man's crotch and says, "Speak or forever hold your piece."

He's So Cool

Fans of James Bond have often said that it is not just what 007 does that makes him so cool, but the way he does it. The average moviegoer can only dream of having the confidence and gumption to do the things that James Bond does. And those that might be so blessed certainly don't have 007's style and panache. Ah, but that's why we're still paying money to see him after all these years. James Bond's five coolest moments are:

1. Bond's introduction in Dr. No

A glamorous young woman, Sylvia Trench (EUNICE GAY-SON), is sitting at a table in a smoky London gaming club, playing baccarat against a man we can't see. After he has

Bond (SEAN CONNERY) introduces himself to the world in Dr. No

won the latest round, the man says to the woman, "I admire your courage, Miss?" "Trench," she sternly replies. "Sylvia Trench. I admire your luck, Mr....?" We now see his face. "Bond," he says. "James Bond." We are seeing James Bond (SEAN CONNERY) on screen for the first time and after this one simple introduction it is obvious that we will never forget him.

2. The tuxedo under the wet suit in Goldfinger

007 (SEAN CONNERY) climbs out of the harbor onto a dock wearing a black wet suit and sneaks into a heroin distribution plant, where he sets the place to blow up. After Bond leaves the plant, he heads towards a local nightclub where he is to meet his contact. But how can he enter the club in a wet suit? No problem. He stands outside the club and unzips the wet suit calmly and matter-of-factly. When Bond peels it off, we see that he is wearing a white dinner jacket underneath!

Did you know that?

There have been three films in the Bond series where James has *not* worn a tuxedo: *From Russia With Love* (remember, that's not James Bond wearing a tux in the pretitle sequence!); *You Only Live Twice*, and *Live and Let Die*.

Did you know that?

James Bond has visited a casino or gambling club in only 10 of the 19 films: *Dr. No; Thunderball; On Her Majesty's Secret Service; Diamonds Are Forever; The Man with the Golden Gun; For Your Eyes Only; Octopussy; Licence To Kill; GoldenEye; The World Is Not Enough.*

To us, he looks perfect. But one thing is missing. Bond reaches into his pocket, pulls out a red carnation and expertly pins it to his breast! Later, the nearby heroin plant explodes and clubgoers scramble out of the club in terror, all except Bond who calmly and coolly puffs on his cigarette in total unconcern.

3. Skeet-shooting in Thunderball

Bond (SEAN CONNERY) is lunching at the seaside home of villain Emilio Largo (ADOLFO CELI). Largo takes Bond near the water to show off his skeet-shooting prowess. After proudly shooting a clay disk out of the air, Largo asks Bond if he would like to try it. Bond takes the gun and says, "It seems terribly difficult." The skeet is then shot into the air, but Bond barely looks at it and, without even raising the rifle, fires a shot from his hip. Of course, the shot shatters the skeet. "No it isn't, is it?" Bond comments smugly to an obviously perturbed Largo.

4. Pheasant-hunting in Moonraker

James Bond (ROGER MOORE) joins villain Hugo Drax' (MICHAEL LONSDALE) hunting party, which is out for a morning shoot on Drax' beautiful northern California estate. Bond

Did you know that?

In the course of the films, James Bond has consumed or ordered a wide range of alcoholic beverages. Some of these include mint julep (*Goldfinger*); rum Collins (*Thunderball*); sake (*You Only Live Twice*); malt whisky and branch water (*On Her Majesty's Secret Service*); sherry (*Diamonds Are Forever*); ouzo (*For Your Eyes Only*); Budweiser with lime (*Licence To Kill*); and bourbon on the rocks (*GoldenEye*). But the vodka martini, shaken, not stirred, is the drink that he is most associated with. In fact, Bond orders, has ordered for him, or is served 14 martinis in the series: *Dr. No* (the porter in his hotel room in Jamaica gives him one and he is given another by Dr. No's waiter near the end of the film); *Goldfinger* (Bond orders one from Mei-Lei on board Goldfinger's jet); *You Only Live Twice* (Bond is given one by Dikko Henderson—mistakenly stirred instead of shaken); *On Her Majesty's Secret Service*

*Mei-Lei (MEI-LING) serves Bond (SEAN CONNERY)
a martini in* Goldfinger

(Marc-Ange Draco orders one for Bond from his secretary); *The Spy Who Loved Me* (Anya orders one for Bond at the Mujava Club in Cairo); *Moonraker* (Manuela makes one for Bond in his hotel room in Rio); *Octopussy* (Octopussy makes one for Bond in her suite); *The Living Daylights* (Bond orders one from the concierge at his hotel in Vienna and Kara makes one for him—spiked with chloral hydrate—in their hotel room in Tangiers); *Licence To Kill* (Bond asks Pam to order him one at the casino is Isthmus City); *GoldenEye* (Bond orders one in the casino in Monte Carlo); *Tomorrow Never Dies* (Paris orders one for Bond at Carver's media party in Hamburg); *The World Is Not Enough* (Bond orders one at the casino in Baku).

007 (ROGER MOORE) doesn't miss in Moonraker

spent the previous night at Drax' mansion, and unbe-
knownst to Bond, Drax is aware that Bond broke into Drax'
safe during that night. The hunting party is winding down
and Drax takes his final shots at the last pheasants. He offers
his gun to Bond to shoot any strays that may fly over. "I
doubt I'm in your class," says Bond. "You're too modest, Mr.
Bond," replies Drax. While this exchange is occurring, one of
Drax' henchmen climbs a tree in the nearby woods, sniper
rifle in hand. A bouquet of pheasants suddenly fly overhead
from the woods. Drax eagerly points them out for Bond and

says "Over there." Bond aims for the pheasants. The sniper sets his sights on Bond. Bond fires. The pheasants continue flying by. "You missed, Mr. Bond," says Drax, hardly containing his glee. Then Bond and Drax see the sniper fall from the tree to the ground, dead. "Did I?" says Bond.

5. The tie adjustment in GoldenEye

James Bond (PIERCE BROSNAN) is at the controls of a Russian T-55 tank rumbling through the streets of St. Petersburg. While eluding half of the Russian army, Bond has destroyed what seems like half of the city as well. At one point he plows right through a very large statue, which comes crashing down unceremoniously on the back of the tank. Only momentarily taken aback by this latest piece of destruction, Bond stops the tank, looks back at the statue, turns around calmly and, before gunning the tank forward, neatly and expeditiously adjusts his tie!

Why Don't They Just Shoot Him?

My 9-year old nephew recently watched his first Bond film. Near the end he uttered a line that many people say when seeing their first Bond film: "I don't understand. If they want to kill him so badly, why don't they just shoot him?" I guess the easy answer is, because then you wouldn't have a Bond film, or a Bond series for that matter! At one point or another probably all of the Bond villains should have just shot Bond. But that would be too boring and would go against the character of these megalomaniacs. No, they've always needed to be creative when attempting to dispatch 007. The five most creative attempts have been:

Bond (SEAN CONNERY) *stares down a laser in* Goldfinger

Did you know that?

Although he has been kicked, punched, beaten, battered, bruised and bloodied, James Bond has only been shot *once* in the entire series: A SPECTRE thug's bullet grazes his ankle as he is escaping from Fiona Volpe's car in *Thunderball*.

1. The laser in Goldfinger

Goldfinger (GERT FROBE) has James Bond (SEAN CONNERY) lying spread-eagled and strapped to a table. Starting be-tweens Bond's feet, a laser slowly burns its way towards Bond's crotch. By some nifty talk, 007 convinces Golfinger that Bond is worth more to him alive than dead. Big mistake.

2. Space shuttle rockets in Moonraker

Hugo Drax (MICHAEL LONSDALE) has left Bond (ROGER MOORE) and Holly Goodhead (LOIS CHILES) trapped under-ground beneath the booster rockets of a space shuttle that is about to lift off! But 007 uses some small explosives and a timer handily hidden in his watch, to blow out the grating of a nearby air shaft. Narrowly escaping the flames of the shuttle rockets, Bond and Holly crawl through it to safety.

3. A coffin in Diamonds Are Forever

An unconscious 007 (SEAN CONNERY) has been placed inside a coffin by the evil duo of Mr. Wint and Mr. Kidd. To make matters worse, the two fiendishly insert the coffin in a crematorium. Bond wakes up to the discomforting realization that he is about to be burned alive. At the last moment, he is bailed out by diamond smugglers Morton Slumber (DAVID BAUER) and Shady Tree (LEONARD BARR), who demand to know where Bond is keeping their diamonds.

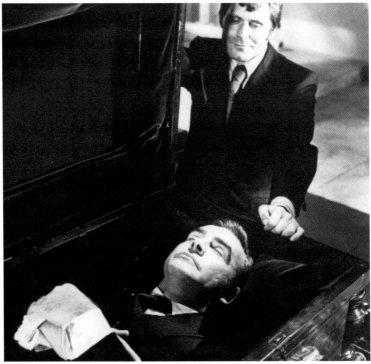

*Mr. Wint (BRUCE GLOVER) gives Bond (SEAN CONNERY)
a proper send-off in* Diamonds Are Forever

4. The torture chair in
The World Is Not Enough

Duplicitous Elektra King (SOPHIE MARCEAU) can't bring herself just to kill Bond (PIERCE BROSNAN) outright. She must tease and torture him first. To do this, she straps Bond into an ancient Turkish torture chair. A wheel in its back, when turned, forces a metal bar slowly into the base of Bond's neck. A few turns and Bond's neck will break. Elektra is one turn from doing just that when she is prevented by the timely arrival of 007's old friend Valentin Zukovsky (ROBBIE COLTRANE), who helps Bond escape.

5. *An atom bomb in Goldfinger*

Goldfinger (GERT FROBE) spared Bond's (SEAN CONNERY) life by not killing him with that laser-beam. Now he has decided that the time is right to send 007 to the afterlife. But no, he doesn't simply shoot him. Instead he handcuffs Bond to an atom bomb that has been set to explode inside Fort Knox. To Goldfinger's chagrin, Bond uses his wits, has some luck and the help of the U.S. Army and avoids being vaporized.

Honorable mention: hanging from the cocaine processor in *Licence To Kill*; hanging above the shark-pool with blood dripping from his arm in *Live and Let Die*.

Bernard Lee as M in Goldfinger

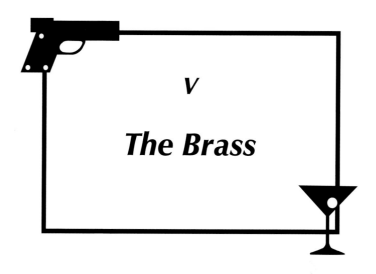

V

The Brass

When all is said and done, James Bond is a loyal servant of Her Majesty's Government. He could never save the world if he didn't have the steadfast support and assistance of the home office back in London. M, Q, and Moneypenny may not always like 007's antics, but deep down you know they all love him! Plus, he makes them and the rest of the British Secret Service (MI6) look pretty good. Now we'll look at the best of M, Q, and Moneypenny scenes.

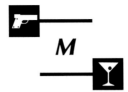

M

007 may be the coolest guy on earth, but as a government agent even he has to answer to someone. Whether M is a man or a woman, he or she may be the only person who isn't afraid to mince words with Bond. And to put him in his place when he needs it. Here are the five best M/007 scenes:

1. Goldfinger

Bond is in for a "dressing down." We've had to wait until the third Bond film, *Goldfinger,* for this moment between 007 and M. (In the first two Bond films, *Dr. No* and *From Russia With Love,* the M/007 scenes serve the standard purpose of M giving 007 his mission and setting up the rest of the movie.) The tension of this "dressing down" lends weight to the scene and gives it the edge that the previous M/007 scenes did not. Bond (SEAN CONNERY) has just returned from Miami, where M (BERNARD LEE) had sent him to observe suspected gold-smuggler Auric Goldfinger. However Bond did more than observe. He interfered with Goldfinger's gin game, causing Goldfinger to lose $15,000, and slept with Goldfinger's assistant, Jill Masterson—Goldfinger promptly has Ms. Masterson killed for her indiscretion. Bond hints to M that he knows who killed Jill, to which M (BERNARD LEE) angrily responds, "This isn't a personal vendetta, 007. It's an assignment like any other. And if you can't treat it as such, coldly and objectively, then 008 can replace you!" A little later Bond and M are at the Bank of England meeting with Colonel Smithers, a gold expert at the bank. During a pause in the meeting Colonel Smithers says, "Have a little more of this rather disappointing brandy." "What's the matter with it?" asks M. At which Bond picks up the bottle of brandy and says, "I'd say it was a 30-year-old fiend indifferently blended." Sniffing from the bottle, Bond adds, "with an overdose of Bombois." This annoys M who retorts, "Colonel Smithers is giving the lecture, 007!"

2. GoldenEye

The "updated Bond of the 90s" needed a new antagonist to deal with. 1995's *GoldenEye,* brought in a female M, played magnificently by Oscar-winner Judi Dench. The new M, just as crusty as the old, has a female perspective on things that clashes with 007's chauvinistic ways. This great scene from *GoldenEye* best illustrates the clash. Bond (PIERCE BROSNAN) has let M know in no uncertain terms that he disagrees with her assessment of the theft of "GoldenEye." Looking Bond in the eyes, M says, "You don't like me, Bond. You don't like my methods. You think I'm an accountant, a bean counter more interested in my numbers than your instincts." "The thought has occurred to me," says Bond. "Good," replies M. "Because I think you're a sexist, misogynist dinosaur. A relic of the cold war whose boyish charms, wasted on me, obviously appealed to that young woman I sent out to evaluate you." "Point taken," says Bond. "Not quite, 007," M snaps. "If you think for one moment I don't have the balls to send a man out to die, your instincts are dead wrong. I've no compunctions about sending you to your death. But I won't do it on a whim, even with your cavalier attitude towards life." As harsh as all of that sounds, at the end of the scene M shows that she does have a soft spot

Judi Dench as M in GoldenEye

for Bond. Leaving the office to begin his search for "Golden-Eye," M says, "Bond, come back alive."

3. *Tomorrow Never Dies*

A British frigate has been sunk off the coast of China. Two Chinese MIGs have been shot down in the same vicinity. The British accuse the Chinese. The Chinese accuse the British. War is imminent. M immediately sends for 007. MI6 has 48 hours to investigate before the shooting starts. It seems a satellite system belonging to media baron Elliot Carver may deliberately have sent the British frigate off course and into Red Chinese waters. The British fleet, already on its way, will reach the Chinese coast in two days. This narrow margin feeds the urgency that causes M (JUDI DENCH) to give Bond (PIERCE BROSNAN) his orders on the run, speeding to the airport in a car with a police escort. They leave the Ministry of Defence and as the car races through traffic, M explains to Bond that he has been added to the invitation list for a party that Carver is hosting that night at his media center in Hamburg. She states bluntly to Bond, "I believe you once had a relationship with Carver's wife, Paris." Surprised, Bond answers, "That was a long time ago, M, before she was married." "Your job is to find out whether Carver or someone in his organization sent that ship off course and why." M pauses, before adding, "Use your relationship with Mrs. Carver, if necessary." Bond replies negatively, "I doubt if she'll remember me." "Remind her," M emphasizes. "Then pump her for information." This is only the second time (*From Russia With Love* being the other) that M has encouraged 007 to use his sexual prowess to enhance a mission's chance of success. Obviously a change of heart for M from the "sexist, misogynist dinosaur," crack in *GoldenEye!*

4. On Her Majesty's Secret Service

The initial M/007 scene in this film is short and to the point; a bluntness that provides the scene's effectiveness. Bond (GEORGE LAZENBY) walks into M's (BERNARD LEE) office and stands in front of his desk. M, head down reading some files, ignores him. Finally, he lifts his head and says, "I'm relieving you from Operation Bedlam, 007." Bond retorts, "But sir, Blofeld's something of a must with me." "You've had two years to run him down," replies M. "Does this mean you've lost confidence in me?" queries Bond. Clearly getting angrier, M, says, "I'm well aware of your talents, 007. Your license to kill is useless unless one can set up a suitable target. I'll find you a more suitable assignment. That's all." Bond attempts to protest, "Sir, under the circumstances..." But M cuts him off sharply, "That's all, that's all!" Bond remains silent, turns around and walks out of the office.

5. Diamonds Are Forever

In *Diamonds Are Forever* the Bond/M scene is not nearly as serious as the one in *On Her Majesty's Secret Service*. Instead, this one is highlighted by a biting, humorous repar-

Did you know that?

M has visited James Bond in the field eight times: *You Only Live Twice* (off the coast of Japan), *The Man with the Golden Gun* (Hong Kong), *The Spy Who Loved Me* (Egypt), *Moonraker* (Venice and Brazil), *A View To A Kill* (Paris), *Licence To Kill* (Key West), *The World Is Not Enough* (Baku).

tee between the two men. It begins at a London diamond syndicate where Bond (SEAN CONNERY) and M (BERNARD LEE) are meeting with the syndicate's head, Sir Donald (LAURENCE NAISMITH). Bond has just returned from abroad where he has finally killed Blofeld (or so he thinks). As Bond and M review some high quality diamonds, Bond says to M, "But surely, sir, there's no reason to bring in our section on a simple smuggling matter." M replies, "Sir Donald's convinced the PM otherwise." Then he crankily adds, "May I remind you, 007, that Blofeld is dead. Finished. The least we can expect from you is some good, solid work." As they all sit down, Sir Donald offers Bond and M some sherry. M declines, citing doctor's orders. Bond gladly accepts and tastes the sherry. He turns to M and says, "Pity about your liver, sir. An unusually fine Solero. '51, I believe." M looks at Bond incredulously and says, "There is no year for sherry, 007."

Bond quickly replies, "I was referring to the original vintage on which the sherry is based." He pauses an instant and says, "1851. Unmistakable." As M looks on in bewilderment, Sir Donald asks 007 what he knows about diamonds. Bond answers, "Hardest substance found in nature, it can cut glass. I suppose they replaced a dog as a girl's best friend," then shrugs as if to say, "That's all I know." M chimes in, "Refreshing to see there's one subject you're not an expert on!" Later, M explains that Bond will be using the cover of Peter Franks, a professional smuggler that MI6 have detained. "Do we know who his contacts are?" asks Bond. An insulted M replies, "We do function in your absence, Commander!"

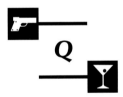

Q, MI6's long-suffering gadget guru (played exclusively by the great Desmond Llewelyn), may be famous the world over, but he still can't get the respect he feels he deserves from James Bond. Even though Q's gadgets have saved 007 many times over, Bond still has major trouble returning these gadgets in "pristine order" when he comes back from the field. According to Q, Bond also has a lot of trouble "paying attention" while Q demonstrates his latest invention.

Will these two ever come to an understanding? I don't know, but it's always fun watching. Of all their scenes together, here are the five best:

1. *Goldfinger*

It isn't until *Goldfinger,* that the Q we all know and love emerges (Q had made a first and brief appearance in *From Russia With Love,* showing up in M's office to supply 007 with his gadget-laden briefcase. This appearance left no lasting impression). The *Goldfinger* scene opens with Bond (SEAN CONNERY) stopping by Q Branch, where Q shows 007 his new Aston Martin DB5 "with modifications" as Q refers to them. Here we encounter the basics of the relationship between the two men: Q, straight-laced and businesslike; Bond, lighthearted and flippant, tweaking Q at every turn. As Q is showing 007 the car's assorted gadgets, Bond rapidly becomes bored. "Is that all?" he asks. Q replies, "I shouldn't keep you for more than an hour or so, if you give me your undivided attention." After Q points out the homing device that will allow Bond to track targets from afar, Bond replies pleasantly, "Allow a man to stop for a quick one en route." Exasperated, Q replies, "It has not been perfected out of years of painstaking research entirely for that purpose, 007." Q requests that Bond turn in the car intact when he returns from the field. Bond reminds Q, "You'd be surprised how much wear and tear goes on out in the field." Q has saved his best item for last: He pops open the top of the gear-lever to reveal "a little red button." "Whatever you do, don't

touch it!" Q warns. Intrigued, Bond asks, "And why not?"
To which Q replies, "Because you'll release and engage the
passenger ejector seat," and even raises his hand to demon-
strate how the device will work. An incredulous 007 replies,
"Ejector seat? You're joking!" At his most serious and stern,
Q states coldly, "I never joke about my work, 007."

2. Tomorrow Never Dies

One of the more amusing of the Q/007 sequences occurs
in *Tomorrow Never Dies*. Bond (PIERCE BROSNAN) arrives at the
airport in Hamburg, walks over to the Avis rental car desk
and inquires about his reservation. The rental agent asks him
to wait and the next moment Q pops up behind him dressed
in a red Avis jacket and says, "If you'd just sign here, Mr.
Bond. It's the insurance damage waiver for your beautiful
new car." Quite surprised at Q's sudden appearance, Bond
gives him an amused grin. "Will you need collision cover-
age?" Q asks holding a waiver form "Yes," Bond replies.
"Fire?" asks Q. "Probably," says Bond. "Property destruction?" continues Q. "Definitely," Bond assures him. "Per-
sonal injury?" asks Q. "I hope not," Bond says, "but
accidents do happen." "They frequently do with you!" sighs
Q. Still amused, Bond signs the waiver and says, "Well, that
takes care of the normal wear and tear. Do I need any other
protection?" "Only from me, 007, unless you bring that car
back in pristine order!" Q retorts. Later, at a hangar in the airport, Q shows Bond his new BMW 750iL. He tries to show
Bond how to steer the car by remote control by using Bond's

new cell phone, but has a hard time controlling it. He points out to Bond just how difficult it is to manage. Bond takes the cell phone and says, "Let's see how she responds to my touch eh, Q?" He then steers the remote controlled car expertly, driving and skidding it around the hangar before steering it towards himself and Q and stopping it only inches in front of them. 007 turns to Q and says, "I think we understand each other." Q shakes his head in dismay at Bond's theatrics and says, "Grow up 007!"

Q *(DESMOND LLEWELYN) gives Bond (PIERCE BROSNAN) a new BMW in* Tomorrow Never Dies

3. *You Only Live Twice*

Unfortunately for Q he is forced to equip Bond on the run again in *You Only Live Twice*. (In the previous film, *Thunderball*, Q had ventured out of MI6 headquarters for the first time to the Bahamas to equip Bond in the field. And he was none too happy about it, explaining to 007, "I must say, I find the idea of equipping you in the field, on the run as it were, highly irregular.") This time he has to travel all the way to Japan to do so. Bond (SEAN CONNERY) has requested the head of the Japanese Secret Service, Tiger Tanaka (TETSURO TAMBA), to contact London and ask them to send "Little Nellie. Suggest she be accompanied by her father. Most urgent." When "Little Nellie" arrives, Tanaka leads Bond into a waiting area where Bond encounters an agitated Q pacing back and forth. "Ah, welcome to Japan, dad," Bond says. "Is my little girl hot and ready?" "Look, 007, I've had a long and tiring journey to no purpose and I'm in no mood for your juvenile quips!" a cranky Q replies. A team of Q Branch assistants quickly assemble "Little Nellie," a small, one-man, autogyro helicopter. Surprised at what he sees, Tanaka asks, "A toy helicopter?" Q immediately defends his creation, stating, "No, it's certainly not a toy! You'll see!" He turns to Bond and says, "We've made one or two improvements since you used her last." The fun ends and Bond and Q get down to business. Little Nellie is wheeled outside and Q gives Bond a quick refresher. "Right. Now pay attention," Q says. "Two machine guns. Fixed." "Synchronized to what?" questions Bond. "One hundred yards. You're using incendiaries and high explosives," Q replies and continues,

"Two rocket launchers. Forward firing on either side." "Fine," Bond says. Q moves along, points to two tubes on the copter and says, "These fire heat-seeking air-to-air missiles. Sixty a minute." "Good," Bond says. Q points to another section of the copter and says, "Flame guns. Two of them. Firing astern." "What range?" asks Bond. "Eighty yards," replies Q. "Two smoke ejectors next door to them," he adds. Moving to the front of Little Nellie, Q says, "Aerial mines. Now, remember, use them only when directly above target. That's about the lot, I think. You know the rest, don't you?" "Yes," a confident Bond replies. Following this scene's lighthearted opening, Q's review of Little Nellie's weapons systems is the most straightforward and businesslike exchange that he and Bond have had in the entire series and a refreshing departure. Of course, Bond shatters this businesslike tone when he takes off in Little Nellie and recklessly flies right over Q's head, which causes Q to cringe at Bond's careless use of government property.

4. Licence To Kill

Bond (TIMOTHY DALTON) and Pam Bouvier (CAREY LOWELL) return to their hotel in Isthmus City, where the concierge informs 007 that his "uncle" has arrived and is waiting in Bond's room. "Your uncle?" a surprised Pam asks. Sensing danger, Bond says to Pam, "Let's make this a proper family reunion. Give me your gun." As they enter the elevator to go up to the room, Pam unzips the bottom of her long evening skirt, unstraps a small gun from her thigh and gives it to Bond. Arriving upstairs, Bond asks Pam to wait outside the room as he prepares to enter and find out just who his "uncle" is. Bond holds up the gun and smashes open the door, which knocks his "uncle" to the ground. Bond points the gun in the man's face, then is shocked to see that his "uncle" is none other than Q! "Really 007!" an equally shocked Q says. A still surprised 007 gasps "Q! What the hell are you doing here?! I might have killed you." "I'm on leave. Thought I'd pop around and see how you're getting on," says Q. "This is no place for you, Q. Go home," Bond says. "Oh, don't be an idiot, 007," Q says. "I know exactly what you're up to. And quite frankly you're going to need my help." He then adds the immortal line, "Remember, if it hadn't been for Q Branch, you'd've been dead long ago." Upon which he pops open his suitcase, saying, "Everything for a man on holiday," and proceeds to demonstrate a laser firing camera, explosive toothpaste, a signature gun, and an "explosive alarm clock, guaranteed never to wake up anyone who uses it." Later, Q does join Bond in the field by chauffeuring him to the building where Bond will attempt to assassinate drug lord Franz Sanchez. Bond thanks Q for his help and pays him the ultimate compliment, in a truly heartfelt manner, "You're a hell of a field operative."

5. The World Is Not Enough

Desmond Llewelyn was tragically killed in a car accident shortly after the release of *The World Is Not Enough*, which makes this final appearance as Q in that film even more poignant than it already is. His encounter with 007 occurs in a Scottish castle, where Q's lab is set up. 007 (PIERCE

BROSNAN) enters the lab and watches a man playing bag-pipes, who turns and fires flames out of the pipes that engulf a target dummy. "I suppose we all have to pay the piper sometime, right, Q?" Bond says. "Oh, pipe down, 007!" says Q. "Is it something I said?" Bond asks. "No!" Q snaps, "Something you destroyed," and he points to the wreckage of the gadget-laden "Q boat," which Bond destroyed in the film's pretitle sequence. "My fishing boat," Q adds, "for my retirement. Away from you." After this exchange, Q introduces Bond to his new assistant (JOHN CLEESE) that will be replacing him. Bond is none too impressed. "You're not retiring anytime soon are you?" a concerned 007 asks Q. "Now pay attention 007," Q says. "I've always tried to teach you two things. First, never let them see you bleed." "And the second?' asks Bond. "Always have an escape plan," says Q as the section of floor that Q is standing on begins to descend slowly, allowing Q to "escape" from the room. As this occurs, Bond and Q share a knowing glance of admiration and respect. A touching send-off.

Moneypenny

Will James Bond and Miss Moneypenny ever get together? Probably not, but watching them tease and needle each other is something audiences look forward to in each film.

Sexual harassment laws haven't cooled these two down. The five most memorable Moneypenny/Bond scenes are:

1. Goldfinger

Having just concluded a discussion with M regarding gold, 007 (SEAN CONNERY) leaves M's office and commences the "customary byplay" (as M calls its) with Moneypenny (LOIS MAXWELL) saying, "Now what do you know about gold, Moneypenny?" Moneypenny flirtatiously replies, "Oh, the only gold I know about is the kind you wear. You know, on the third finger of your left hand." Bond casually replies, "You know, one of these days we must really look into that." Moneypenny perks up and says, "Well, what about tonight? You come around for dinner and I'll cook you a beautiful

Did you know that?

Miss Moneypenny meets with 007 outside of MI6's London Headquarters on six occasions: *You Only Live Twice* (on M's submarine); *On Her Majesty's Secret Service* (at James Bond's wedding in Spain); *Diamonds Are Forever* (at the Hovercraft station); *Live and Let Die* (at James Bond's flat); *The Spy Who Loved Me* (at M's office in Egypt); *A View To A Kill* (at the Ascot races).

angel cake." "Oh, nothing would give me greater pleasure," says Bond. "But, unfortunately, I do have a business appointment." Frowning, Moneypenny says, "That's the flimsiest excuse you've ever given me. Ah well, some girls have all the luck. Who is she, James?" Before Bond can answer, the intercom on Moneypenny's desk blares and we hear M's voice, "She is me, Miss Moneypenny. And kindly omit the customary byplay with 007. He's dining with me and I don't want him to be late." This news brings an instant smile to Moneypenny's face. "So there's hope for me yet?" she asks Bond. Bond leans in, gives her a soft kiss on the cheek and says, "Moneypenny, won't you ever believe me?"

2. GoldenEye

007's relationship with the long-suffering Moneypenny changed dramatically in the 90s, as did his relationship with M. It changed enough that Moneypenny can no longer be called "long-suffering." Sure, she still wants Bond, but this scene from *GoldenEye* shows a shift in the balance of power in their relationship that finally puts the two on a more equal footing. Bond (PIERCE BROSNAN) says "Good evening, Moneypenny," as he enters Moneypenny's (SA-MANTHA BOND) office. "Good evening, James. M will meet you in the situation room. I'm to take you straight in," she responds. Bond notices that Moneypenny is dressed to the nines and says, "I've never seen you after hours, Moneypenny. Lovely." She smiles and says, "Thank you, James." "Out on some kind of professional assignment, dressing to kill?"questions Bond. "I know you'll find this crushing,

007," Moneypenny replies, "but I don't sit at home every night praying for some international incident, so I can run down here all dressed up to impress James Bond. I was on a date, if you must know, with a gentleman. We went to the theatre together." Bond feigns disappointment and says "Moneypenny, I'm devastated. What would I ever do without you?" "As far as I can remember, James," Moneypenny responds, "you've never had me." "Hope springs eternal," says Bond. "You know, this sort of behavior would qualify for sexual harassment," says Moneypenny. Increasingly amused, Bond asks "Really? What's the penalty for that?" "Some day you have to make good on your innuendoes," says a defiant Moneypenny.

3. *Tomorrow Never Dies*

The witty Bond and Moneypenny repartee continues in the next film, *Tomorrow Never Dies*. A romantic interlude between a luscious Danish language professor at Oxford and Bond (PIERCE BROSNAN) is rudely interrupted when Bond's cell phone rings. He finds the phone on the floor and hears Moneypenny (SAMANTHA BOND) say, "James? Where are you?" Bond answers, "Oh, Moneypenny I'm just up here at Oxford brushing up on a little Danish." Moneypenny replies, "I'm afraid you're going to have to kiss off your lesson, James, we've got a situation here at the Ministry of Defense. We're sending the fleet to China." "I'll be there in an hour," acknowledges Bond. "Make that thirty minutes," she retorts. At which Bond turns to the blond professor and says in Danish "Goodbye my sweet" as he kisses her. Moneypenny, is still listening and comments, "You always were a cunning linguist, James."

4. On Her Majesty's Secret Service

Moneypenny (LOIS MAXWELL) does more than flirt with Bond (GEORGE LAZENBY) in this movie, she helps save his job. Their scene together starts off in the usual manner with Bond entering Moneypenny's office. "James! Where have you been?" she asks. "Much too far from you, darling," he replies as he leans over and kisses her on the cheek. "Same old James," a smiling Moneypenny says. But Bond then surprises her by pinching her on the backside. "Only more so!" a shocked Moneypenny adds. "Heartless Brute, letting me pine away without even a postcard!" "Pine no more," Bond soothes her. "Cocktails at my place. Eightish. Just the two of us." "Oh, I'd adore that," she replies, "if only I could trust myself!" "Same old Moneypenny! Britain's last line of defense!" says Bond and heads into M's office. A few minutes later he comes out and shocks Moneypenny again by asking her to draft his resignation letter to M. Bond is angry that M has removed him from Operation Bedlam, the search for Blofeld. Later when M accepts the request, stating "Request granted," it shocks Bond that M has accepted his resignation so easily. He turns to Moneypenny to talk about it; she asks him to open the "resignation" letter that she wrote for him. He sees that it requests "Two weeks leave." She smiles at the perplexed Bond and says, "You didn't really want to resign, did you?" Bond smiles in acknowledgement. "Moneypenny," he says affectionately, "What would I do without

Lois Maxwell as Miss Moneypenny in You Only Live Twice

you?" "My problem is, you never do anything with me!" she answers back. After Bond leaves, the office intercom blares and M's voice says, "What would I do without you, Miss Moneypenny. Thank you!"

5. You Only Live Twice

Moneypenny (LOIS MAXWELL) looks her most fetching of the series in this film. Aboard a Royal Navy submarine off the coast of Japan, Bond (SEAN CONNERY) comes to an office cabin where he finds Moneypenny sitting behind a desk just as she would back at Headquarters in London. In her naval whites, we've never seen her looking better. Bond completes his briefing with M, then Moneypenny gives him the password he will need when he meets up with the Japanese Secret Service. "I love you," she says to Bond slowly and suggestively. In an attempt to have Bond say the words that she has longed to hear, she says "Repeat it please, so you don't forget it." But 007 dissappoints her with, "Don't worry. I get it." Moneypenny frowns and, as he is leaving, she tosses a small book at him, which he catches. He reads the title, "Instant Japanese," and smiles. "You forget I took a first in oriental languages at Cambridge," he reminds a very impressed Moneypenny.

Moneypenny gets her revenge on 007 at the end of the film, when Bond and Japanese agent Kissy Suzuki are floating in a raft on the ocean. Hardly have they got amorous, than M's submarine emerges from the water right beneath the raft. Inside the submarine M turns to Moneypenny and orders her, "Tell him to come below and report." Moneypenny smiles devilishly and says, "It'll be a pleasure, sir."

Sean Connery and the Aston Martin DB5 from Goldfinger

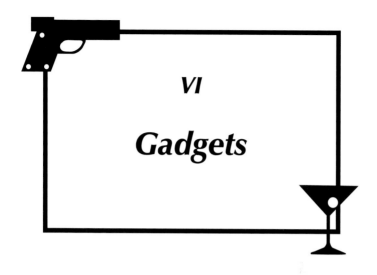

VI

Gadgets

Felix Leiter assembles a host of gadgets for James Bond to use in the finale of *Thunderball*. Bond, surprised by this array of deadly toys he has been given, quips, "and the kitchen sink." But it is these toys that have kept him alive this long. Whether they be large gadgets, like specially rigged motor-boats and sports cars, or smaller gadgets, like laser-firing watches and exploding pens, it is the gadgets Q Branch gives 007 that provides his decided advantage over his opponents. Isn't it just too bad for the rest of us that none of these "toys" have ever been put on the market? As usual, James Bond has all the fun!

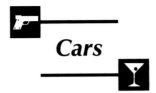

Cars

There probably isn't a person alive who at one time or another hasn't wished that they had one of James Bond's cars. When we're stuck in bad traffic, wouldn't it relieve stress if we could fire rockets at the cars in front of us? Or slash the tires of the car beside us? Or how about using an ejector seat to project the passenger, who won't shut up, out of the car and onto the road? James Bond can do all of those things! The five coolest Bond cars are:

1. Aston Martin DB5 in Goldfinger

James Bond's silver Aston Martin DB5 would be a pretty damn cool car under any circumstances. But it is the "modifications" (as Q refers to them) that make it exceptional. These modifications include front-mounted machine guns, an oil slick, tire-slashing buzz saws, a homing device (to allow one to "stop for a quick one en route," as Bond (SEAN CONNERY) explains to a disgruntled Q), and the piece de resistance, a passenger ejector seat! Bond's use of each of these tools to systematically dispatch his pursuers makes the Aston Martin chase in *Goldfinger* one of the best to watch in the series. No wonder the DB5 earned the title "The Most Famous Car in the World." Because of its popularity it showed up in the next Bond film, *Thunderball*, and over 30 years later in *GoldenEye* and *Tomorrow Never Dies*.

2. Lotus Esprit in The Spy Who Loved Me

Could the producers of the Bond films find an adequate replacement for the Aston Martin DB5? After 13 years, they finally did in *The Spy Who Loved Me*: A white Lotus Esprit that

The Lotus Esprit in The Spy Who Loved Me

takes 007's gadgetry to a new level. Rocket launchers and a gun that shoots mud at the windshields of pursuing vehicles are only warm-ups for this car's real attraction—it turns into a fully operational submarine! Watching Bond (ROGER MOORE) use his new submersible is pure fun and one of the more visually exciting set pieces of the series. Yet Soviet agent Anya Amasova (BARBARA BACH) is not impressed. She nonchalantly tells Bond, "I saw the blueprints for this car two years ago."

3. BMW 750iL in *Tomorrow Never Dies*

As sleek and classy as the BMW 750iL is, a luxury sedan and not a sports car is not your typical Bond car. But its unique feature, that it can be driven by remote control, is used to great effect by Bond (PIERCE BROSNAN) in evading Carver's thugs in a parking garage. Aside from its own assortment of rocket launchers, it also features tires that re-inflate themselves after being punctured. Another highlight: the windows are impervious to sledgehammers!

Did you know that?

Only two of the cars that Q has given 007 over the years have been returned to him in one piece: The Lotus Esprit in *The Spy Who Loved Me* (damaged, but still in one piece) and the BMW Z3 Roadster in *GoldenEye*.

4. *Aston Martin DB7 in The Living Daylights*

23 years after the original appeared, Bond receivs a brand-new 1987 model Aston Martin for *The Living Daylights*. It is every bit as impressive as its illustrious predecessor, with rocket launchers replacing the machine guns behind the headlights. And it doesn't matter that Bond (TIMOTHY DALTON) is forced to drive on ice and snow because it comes equipped with skis!

5. *BMW Z3 Roadster in GoldenEye*

Okay, the BMW Z3 in *GoldenEye* is strictly a product placement and therefore we don't see Bond use any of its modifications, like those stinger missiles that Q mentions. But the car is damn good looking and Pierce Brosnan's Bond looks just as good driving it along a dirt road in Puerto Rico. Probably the only person who is happy that this car doesn't see any action is Q—at least it came back to him intact from the field!

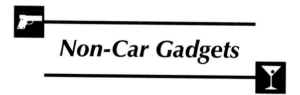

Non-Car Gadgets

"Boys with toys," who better represents this expression than James Bond? No boy out there has had more, or better, toys than Bond. Now we know that 007 has had his share of gadget-laden cars, but it is the capability of other gadgets that has saved his life many times over. Q once told Bond, "If it hadn't been for Q Branch, you'd've been dead long ago (*Licence To Kill*)" Here are the five best non-car gadgets that have enabled Bond to still be with us:

1. The AcroStar Bede minijet in Octopussy

A one-man jet airplane—the AcroStar Bede minijet from *Octopussy*, which folds up enough to sit hidden in the back of a horse trailer—has to be James Bond's most impressive non-car gadget. Bond (ROGER MOORE) has just failed in his attempt to blow up an airplane hangar in an unnamed, communist Latin American country. Arriving to rescue him, his assistant, Bianca (TINA HUDSON), drives over from a nearby horse show in a small truck with a horse trailer attached. As the army of this unnamed country bears down on them, Bond climbs out of the truck onto the trailer, which he detaches. Army vehicles are racing toward the trailer, when the faux horse hindquarters visible at the rear of the trailer pop open and a minijet with Bond at the controls rolls out. The wings unfold and Bond races the jet down the highway right at the on-coming military, narrowly missing the vehicles as he lifts off. As Bond shoots skyward, the soldiers launch a heat-seeking missile which hones directly on his jet. The amazing little plane zigs and zags sideways and up and down, but can't shake the missile. Finally, Bond sees a chance: the airplane hangar he had been sent to destroy, with its doors wide open, is ahead. He

007 (ROGER MOORE) pilots the AcroStar jet in Octopussy

descends and aims the jet at the opening. The plane sweeps through the doors causing shocked mechanics and crewmen to scramble. They are hastily ordered to close the doors on the far side to prevent Bond's escape. As they begin to do this, 007's amazing little machine turns sideways and slips through and out of the hangar, barely missing the closing doors. The missile that has followed him into the hangar slams into the now closed doors. Destroyed: one hangar. Saved: one soaring James Bond.

2. Wrist-darts in Moonraker

Villain Hugo Drax (MICHAEL LONSDALE) corners James Bond (ROGER MOORE) on board his space station and points

Bond (ROGER MOORE) receives poison darts from Q (DESMOND LLEWELYN) in Moonraker

his laser gun at Bond. He says, "Desolated, Mr. Bond." Raising his hand slowly to surrender, Bond flicks his right wrist and shoots a poison dart out from under his shirt cuff that lands in Drax's chest. "Heartbroken, Mr. Drax," replies Bond. 007 had just been been saved by a wrist-dart firing mechanism that Q had given him. The quick flick of the wrist to which it is strapped shoots a poison dart out. Q supplied Bond with 10 darts, "5 blue-tipped causing unconsciousness, and 5 red-tipped causing death in 30 seconds." "Very novel, Q," says Bond. "You must get them in the stores for Christmas."

3. Key ring in The Living Daylights

Q gives 007 a key ring that has a basic feature of many: it beeps when you whistle. But since this is a Q-Branch key ring, it has a couple of special features: If you whistle the first four bars of "Rule Britannia," the ring emits stun gas; if you whistle a "Wolf Whistle," it explodes! Bond (TIMOTHY DALTON) uses the first as he is about to be thrown in a Soviet prison in Afghanistan. He whistles the first four bars of "Rule Britannia", and the stun gas disorients the guards just long enough for Bond to overpower them and escape. Near the end of the film, villain Brad Whitaker (JOE DON BAKER) corners the out-of-ammo Bond hiding behind a large bust of British general Wellington in his military museum. Machine-gun in hand, Whitaker creeps in front of the bust, ready for the kill. Before he can fire, Bond takes out his key ring, attaches it to the back of the bust (the key ring is also magnetic!) and wolf whistles. The key ring explodes, causing the bust of Wellington to topple on Whitaker and crush him.

4. X-ray vision sunglasses in The World Is Not Enough

James Bond fulfills every red-blooded male's fantasy in *The World Is Not Enough* when he wears X-ray vision sunglasses that allow him to see through clothing. Going into the casino in Baku, Bond (PIERCE BROSNAN) puts on the glasses so that he can see which of the dubious-looking patrons and employees are armed, and sees that just about every person in the place is carrying some kind of weapon beneath their clothing. But what makes these glasses so special for 007, is they allow him to check out the skimpy lingerie (or lack thereof) of the attractive female patrons. The look on Bond's face as he eyes up one unsuspecting beauty after another is priceless. Can one doubt that these glasses may be the one gadget Bond can find use for when he is off duty?

5. Jet pack in Thunderball

Some may say that James Bond is a kind of superman. Well, the jet pack in *Thunderball* allowed Bond to mimic the superhero by literally flying away from his pursuers. Bond (SEAN CONNERY) must escape from the French chateau where he has killed SPECTRE agent Jacques Boivard (BOB SIMMONS). He runs onto a balcony where a one-man jet pack is waiting to aid his escape. Bond straps the twin-tanked pack to his back, wraps his hands around the controls, and blasts off into the air as his pursuers look on in awe. Using the controls, he flies up and away from the chateau before maneuvering downwards to make a perfect soft landing on his feet right next to his Aston Martin. Bond and his waiting lady-friend load the jet pack into the car's trunk, and he quips, "No well-dressed man should be without one."

Honorable mention: the briefcase in *From Russia With Love*; the belt in *GoldenEye*; the inflatable jacket in *The World Is Not Enough*.

Q Lab Gadgets

Not every ingenious gadget created by Q Branch makes it into the hands of 007. Some are, as Q likes to point out, "not perfected yet." And some just wouldn't be practical for Bond (an arm-cast that springs open to smash your neighbor's head? I don't think Bond would look stylish with a cast on his arm). But, whenever 007 takes a tour through Q's laboratory (which can be located in places as far off as Egypt, Brazil or India), Q always has a bevy of interesting gadgets to show off. Five of the best gadgets that didn't reach the field:

1. The ghetto blaster from
The Living Daylights

Bond (TIMOTHY DALTON) is about to leave Q Branch when one of Q's assistants pops up holding a boombox. He hoists it on his shoulder and directs it towards a target dummy. By pushing a button, a rocket is fired that blows the target dummy to pieces. "Something we're making for the Americans," Q explains. "It's called a ghetto blaster."

2. The tea tray from The Spy Who Loved Me

In Q's Lab in Egypt, Bond (ROGER MOORE) and Q pass an assistant who is placing a tea tray at one end of a table. A target dummy sits at the other end. When the assistant holds the tray just above a table place setting, it shoots out of his hand, flies the length of the table and decapitates the dummy. "I want that ready for Achmed's tea party," Q tells

Did you know that?

Aside from MI6 Headquarters in London, Q-Branch laboratories have been found in four other locations: Egypt in *The Spy Who Loved Me*; Brazil in *Moonraker*; India in *Octopussy*; and Scotland in *The World Is Not Enough*.

his assistant soberly. We can only guess who poor Achmed might be and be thankful that we're not invited to his party!

3. The couch in The Living Daylights

Q asks an assistant to lie down on what looks to be a very comfortable couch. The man does and disappears without a trace, swallowed between the cushions and the back of the couch!

4. The telephone booth in GoldenEye

A Q Lab assistant stands in a telephone booth holding the receiver. Bond (PIERCE BROSNAN) and Q watch as an air bag opens and inflates and traps the hapless assistant against the booth's glass window.

5. The umbrella in For Your Eyes Only

A Q Lab dummy holds an umbrella over its head. From above the dummy, an assistant pours water onto the umbrella, which causes the umbrella to sprout daggers and collapse around the dummy's head. "Stinging in the rain?" Bond (ROGER MOORE) asks Q.

Honorable mention: the bowlers in *Moonraker*; the leg-cast in *GoldenEye*; the bagpipes in *The World Is Not Enough*.

Bond (ROGER MOORE) goes on the attack in The Spy Who Loved Me

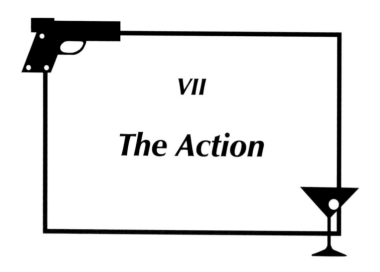

VII

The Action

Many elements have contributed to the success of the James Bond films over the years. Audiences expect the staples of romance, sex, humor, great locations, great sets and memorable characters. But at their heart, Bond films always have been and always will be action/adventure films. Action/adventure is the core ingredient of each film. Chases, stunts, shootouts, fistfights, explosions and hair-raising escapes are what make the Bond films the edge-of-your-seat thrillers that they are. This following section highlights the best action of the series.

Pretitle Sequences

Notice that hardly anyone shows up late for a Bond film in the theater. That's because everyone knows that the Bond pretitle or "teaser" sequences can be the most exciting and jaw-dropping scenes in the whole movie. Mini-movies in themselves, these sequences often find Bond in the middle of a precarious situation or at the end of a not-seen mission. Evolving over the years from small fight scenes to globe-trotting set pieces that end with an edge-of-your-seat, death-defying stunt, these "teasers" usually leave a big smile on the audiences' faces. The five best that tease us are:

1. Goldfinger

007 (SEAN CONNERY) emerges from the harbor in a wet suit onto a dock. He promptly dispatches a guard and sneaks into what appears to be a large water tank, but is in fact a stylishly furnished apartment that houses barrels of heroin-flavored bananas. Bond quickly covers the barrels with plastic explosives and sets a timer. He quietly creeps out of the tank and begins to shed his wet suit. We see that 007 is wearing a tuxedo underneath the suit (a trick that James Cameron and Arnold Schwarzenegger copy years later in their Bond homage, *True Lies*). 007 then enters a nearby night-club. He checks his watch and.....BAM!, the explosives go

off, destroying the tank and the heroin. The patrons of the nightclub scatter in confusion, while Bond calmly makes his contact. The man informs Bond that a plane is leaving for Miami in one hour. "I'll be on it," says Bond, "but first I have some unfinished business to attend to." We cut to Bond's hotel room where he finds his girl waiting in the tub for him. As they kiss, an assassin (ALF JOINT) comes behind Bond wielding a club. Bond sees the man reflected in the girl's eyes and uses the girl as a shield to deflect the blow from the club. A rough-and-tumble fight ensues, which ends when Bond flings the man into the tub followed by a live electric heater. Seeing the electrocuted assassin Bond comments, "Shocking, positively shocking." Before the credits have even rolled, the audience has been treated to intrigue (Bond sneaking into the tank), destruction (Bond blowing up the tank), sex (Bond kissing a half-naked woman), action (the fight between Bond and the assassin) and humor (Bond's parting one-liner). Handled with style and panache, each of these elements add up to make this the best Bond teaser sequence.

Did you know that?

Four times a pretitle sequence has ended with Bond using a parachute to escape: *The Spy Who Loved Me; Moonraker; The Living Daylights; Licence To Kill.*

2. *The Spy Who Loved Me*

The movie stuntwork in the pretitle sequence of *The Spy Who Loved Me* raised the bar and forever changed the course of such sequences in the Bond series. Where previous pretitles, following *Goldfinger's* lead, usually comprised a scene with Bond in a rousing punch-up with some baddies, *The Spy Who Loved Me's* sequence is a mini-movie in itself. A British submarine disappears under mysterious circumstances. A cut to the Kremlin shows General Gogol getting a message off to his best agent, Triple X. Next a scene in M's office, has him asking Moneypenny (LOIS MAXWELL) anxiously where 007 is. "He's on mission, sir. In Austria," she replies. "Well tell him to pull out," says M (BERNARD LEE). We find Bond (ROGER MOORE) in an Austrian ski chalet making love to a beautiful woman. A ticker-tape message to report to Headquarters immediately comes over his watch. Before we know it, Bond is out of the chalet and skiing down the slopes. Several Soviet agents on skis, alerted by the woman, set upon 007 and chase him down the mountain, firing machine-guns as they go. By activating his rocket-firing ski pole 007 kills one of his pursuers, but the others continue to close in on him. The bad situation deteriorates as we see that Bond is heading towards a cliff; and he continues towards the cliff edge and skis right off it. And he falls and falls and falls some more, until at last he pulls a ripcord and a parachute unfurls. Audiences in 1977 (myself included) had never seen a stunt anything like it before in movie history, and it stands as one of the greatest stunts of all time—and contributes to making the teaser from *The Spy Who Loved Me* so great.

3. Octopussy

007 is captured while trying to blow up an aircraft hangar in an unnamed Latin American country. As Bond (ROGER MOORE) is being led away, his female assistant, Bianca (TINA HUDSON), helps him escape. With the country's army bearing down on him, Bond hops into his small, one-man minijet that has been hidden in a horse trailer. He takes off in the jet and seems to be in the clear, until a heat-seeking air-to-air missile is fired at him. As the missile pursues Bond's jet, Bond zigs and zags the little plane up, down, sideways, and even upside-down, but he cannot evade it. Time seems to be running out, when Bond sees a chance. He puts the jet in a dive and heads straight for the aircraft hangar that he had been sent to destroy. The missile is still on his tail as Bond's jet enters the open hangar and barnstorms its way through and out the other end, barely squeaking out between the closing doors. But the following missile doesn't make it. It crashes into the hangar and causes a massive explosion. Mission accomplished!

Did you know that?

Three times 007 ended a pretitle sequence at the controls of a plane: *Octopussy; GoldenEye; Tomorrow Never Dies.*

007 (SEAN CONNERY) gets cuffed in Thunderball

4. Thunderball

SPECTRE agent Jacques Boivard (BOB SIMMONS), who had murdered two of Bond's colleagues, is being buried. As the funeral ends, Bond (SEAN CONNERY) notices Boivard's veil-covered widow rush to her limousine, ignoring the chauffeur, and open the door for herself. Cut. The widow Boivard enters a nearby French chateau and sees a man sitting in a guest chair. None other than James Bond. 007 walks over to the surprised woman and says, "Madam, I'm here to offer my sincere condolences." He then punches her in the face. Off come her veil and wig to reveal Jacques Boivard himself, very much alive. The two struggle furiously with fists, vases, credenzas, curtains and finally a fireplace poker, which Bond uses to strangle Boivard. But the danger is not over, as Bond leaves the room with Boivard's henchmen giving chase. 007 climbs out to a balcony where he has left a small trinket—a Bell-Textrow jet pack. He straps on the jet pack and shoots himself into the air, leaving a group of befuddled pursuers. Bond maneuvers himself away from the chateau and lands in the street near his waiting Aston Martin. His female assistant helps him load the jet pack in the car's trunk before they jump in the car. Gunshots from more approaching henchmen cause Bond to raise the Aston's bullet shield and then turn a lever that shoots water at the oncoming goons. The main titles begin to roll, as the water shoots into frame.

5. The World Is Not Enough

By far the longest teaser of the series (14 minutes), this pretitle is actually three sequences rolled into one. It begins with Bond (PIERCE BROSNAN) in a Swiss banker's office in Bilbao, Spain, where 007 has been sent to retrieve some stolen money and find some information regarding a dead British agent. The meeting turns sour and Bond has to kill or beat up the banker's thugs. To get the information he needs he holds a gun to the banker's head, but the banker is killed by a knife thrown by his beautiful assistant, "the cigar girl"

Bond (PIERCE BROSNAN) escapes in The World Is Not Enough

(MARIA GRAZIA CUCINOTTA). As the cigar girls escapes, Bond hears the local authorities heading for the office. Holding one end of a curtain wire and weighting the other with the body of one of the beaten-up thugs, Bond jumps out of the office window and rappells down to the street. The pretitle cuts to MI6 Headquarters in London, where Bond turns over the money and then heads up to M's office, where he meets a British oil tycoon, Sir Robert King, whose money he has just retrieved. King departs and Bond and M (JUDI DENCH) sit down for a drink. When Bond happens to touch the ice in his drink, it begins to sizzle. He realizes that there must be a chemical residue on his fingers and it came from the money he touched and that money is going to explode! Bond dashes out of M's office to stop King from picking up the money, but he is too late. The money explodes the instant King touches it, causing major damage to MI6 Headquarters. Bond peers out through the gaping hole in the side of the building and sees a woman—the cigar girl!—in a boat on the Thames. She fires a machine gun at him and takes off in her boat. Bond rushes to Q Branch, where over Q's protests, he hops into Q's new gadget-laden mini-speedboat, rockets the boat out of the side of the building, through the air, and into the river. The ensuing boat chase, with 007 dodging bullets and grenades from the cigar girl, races not only down the Thames, but under it, over it, onto nearby streets, and back onto the water. Bond fires two torpedoes right for the cigar girl's boat as she heads for the riverbank. They strike and destroy it, but the girl jumps clear. She finds herself in front of Britain's then-new Millennium Dome where a hot-air balloon is set to launch. She hops into the balloon gondola and lifts off. Bond's speed-boat shoots out of the water towards the balloon; he jumps out and grabs one of the balloon's dangling mooring lines as the balloon rises. The girl shoots at him as he hangs below her. Two police helicopters appear, and the cigar girl realizes she is trapped. Bond pleads with her to give herself up, but she ignores him and fires her gun at the balloon helium-tank, which ignites and she and the balloon go up in flames. Bond falls away and eventually lands on the roof of the Dome. He tumbles over and over before he finally catches hold of one of the Dome's suspension cables. Once again we see 007 hanging on for dear life as the main titles roll—ending a sequence with more action, twists and turns than most movies.

Honorable mention: *On Her Majesty's Secret Service; Moonraker; Licence To Kill; GoldenEye; Tomorrow Never Dies.*

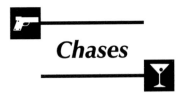

Chases

Chase sequences have always been one of the hallmarks of the Bond series. No 007 movie is complete without one or two good ones and since anything goes in a Bond film, these chases take place not only on the ground, but on the water and in the air as well (sometimes, all three!). While cars are the vehicle of choice in these chases 007 has also used the following modes of transport while chasing or being chased: speedboats, helicopters, skis, moon buggies, double-decker buses, gondolas, airplanes, firetrucks, tanker trucks, tanks, motorcycles, and even a cello case! Anything he can get his hands on at the moment of need! The five most exciting chases are:

1. The Aston Martin chase in *Goldfinger*

This chase is an excuse to showcase the car's wonderful gadgets, as if an excuse were needed! At the same time, it establishes the formula that most of the series' chase sequences would follow: Bond in some sort of vehicle being chased by multiple assailants in multiple vehicles, with only his wits and some well-placed gadgets to aid him. In *Goldfinger*, 007 (SEAN CONNERY) uses the Aston Martin's oil slick, smoke screen, machine guns, bullet-proof shield and the *piece de resistance*—the passenger ejector seat—to evade, dispatch and befuddle Goldfinger's heavies, who are chasing him along the dark forest roads that surround "Auric Enterprises," Goldfinger's base in Switzerland. The sequence expertly combines excitement, drama, humor, and terror (when Odd Job uses his steel-rimmed bowler hat to murder Bond's companion, Tilly Masterson). For an example of a Bond chase sequence, you couldn't choose a better scene than this.

2. The speedboat chase in Live and Let Die

Live and Let Die elevates the humorous approach of the car chase in the previous film, *Diamonds Are Forever*. In that movie, local police chase Bond through the streets of Las Vegas. Now, 007 (ROGER MOORE) escapes by speedboat from

007 (ROGER MOORE) flees via speedboat in Live and Let Die

villain Kananga's alligator farm and is chased through Louisiana bayou country, a chase featuring some of the best stuntwork in the series. The liberal dose of humor is delivered by Sheriff J.W. Pepper (CLIFTON JAMES) of the Louisiana State Police (or po-lice, as J.W. refers to it), who is chasing Bond as well as the villains are. The frustrated Sheriff's use in the scene is played strictly for laughs, and borders on slapstick, but the daring stuntwork more than makes up for this shortfall. Watching the various speedboats zigzag their way through the bayous at high speed as well as fly through the air over water, roads and cars gives plenty of thrills. This sequence was the precursor of some stunt-laden chases that would follow later in the series and it is the highlight of *Live and Let Die.*

3. The Lotus Esprit chase in
The Spy Who Loved Me

007's Lotus Esprit is laden with gadgets, like the Aston Martin in *Goldfinger*, but this chase ratchets things up by taking the vehicle to air and sea as well. Bond (ROGER MOORE) and Soviet agent Anya Amasova (BARBARA BACH) are being closely pursued along a cliff-road in Sardinia by thugs in a car and on a motorcycle with sidecar. No sooner have Bond and Anya dispatched their pursuers than they are attacked from the air by the evil Naomi (CAROLINE MUNRO) firing machine guns from a helicopter. The machine-gun fire forces Bond to race the Lotus off a quay, into the air, and into the Mediterranean. But have no fear—the Lotus turns into a fully functional submersible! As Naomi hovers above, 007 fires a missile from the Lotus that sends the copter and Naomi to a fiery death. But Bond and Anya are not "out of the water" yet. Using the submersible, Bond spies on villain Karl Stromberg's underwater lair, Atlantis, but is set upon by rocket-firing frogmen and a two-man sub. But the Lotus' arsenal saves the day. A rocket and a mine make short work of the attackers, after which the besieged Lotus makes it to shore and drives up the beach, astonishing the local sunbathers.

4. The BMW 750IL chase in *Tomorrow Never Dies*

After the wide-ranging Lotus Esprit chase in *The Spy Who Loved Me* over the local Sardinian geography, the confines of 007's BMW chase in *Tomorrow Never Dies* must be the tightest ever: a multistory parking garage in Hamburg. The tight lanes of the packed garage force Bond (PIERCE BROSNAN) to maneuver fast and skillfully while being fired at by Carver's hitmen using machine guns and rocket launchers, and all while steering from his remote control and slumped across the back-seat! He needs the help of all the BMW's "special features" in this situation—rockets, metal tacks (to puncture the tires of his pursuers), bullet-proof windows and chassis, metal-cutter and re-inflatable tires—to survive his attackers' withering fire. Finally Bond dives out from the back of the car, while continuing to drive it by remote control and his pursuers are left chasing an empty car!

5. The tanker truck chase in Licence To Kill

At the finale of *Licence To Kill*, the size of the vehicles involved stands out. Bond (TIMOTHY DALTON) doesn't have the luxury of driving a gadget-laden sports car. Instead he is behind the wheel of an 18-wheel oil-tanker, and he is doing the chasing. With no gadgets to fall back on, Bond must use his wits and his considerable driving skills to negotiate a mountain road in Latin America. These skills en-

Bond (TIMOTHY DALTON) "drives" an oil-tanker in Licence To Kill

able Bond to drive the 18-wheeler on nine wheels, tipped to its side, to avoid an oncoming missile fired by the villains: truly a highlight of the sequence. As 007's truck rights itself, it lands smack on top of the villains' Jeep and crushes it. Later he disengages the oil tank from the driving-cab, jettisoning the tank down the mountain where it smashes into one of the other tankers that he is chasing. Lots of explosions, dust, screeching tires and twisted metal—a chase to remember!

Honorable mention: The Mustang chase in *Diamonds Are Forever*; The Aston Martin chase in *The Living Daylights;* The tank chase in *GoldenEye*.

Did you know that?

James Bond has risked his life hanging from a flying machine 10 times: *For Your Eyes Only* (helicopter); *Octopussy* (airplane); *A View To A Kill* (blimp); *The Living Daylights* (airplane); *Licence To Kill* (2 airplanes *and* a helicopter); *GoldenEye* (airplane *and* helicopter); *The World Is Not Enough* (hot-air balloon).

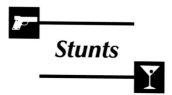

Stunts

No Bond film would be complete without a couple of death-defying stunts and it's been daunting for the producers to top what has come before, as the series has progressed. Amazingly though, they have frequently been up to the task. Here are the five best stunts of the series:

1. Bond and Necros hanging from the plane in The Living Daylights

Bond (TIMOTHY DALTON) and Necros (ANDREAS WISNIEW-SKI) are battling it out in the back of a Soviet transport plane, while Kara Milovy (MARYAM D'ABO) is at the controls. She mistakenly pulls the lever that opens the rear of the plane and Bond and Necros are sucked towards the back. Luckily for them the plane is filled with sacks of opium which are tied down in netting. Bond and Necros slide toward the rear opening and the large netting filled with the sacks slides with them, so they both jump onto it. They hang on to the huge bundle as it slides out of the back of the plane, drops and hangs there, caught, as the plane flies on. As they fight, Bond cuts away the sacks of opium with a knife and now they must fight with the sacks flying in their faces. Bond eventually sends Necros falling to his death. Because the weight of the sacks and of Necros is gone, the wind flings the netting and Bond back into the plane! All-in-all a remarkable three-part stunt.

2. *Bond skiing off the cliff in The Spy Who Loved Me*

Not only did this stunt change the Bond series forever, it upped the ante for stuntwork in the entire film industry. Soviet agents on skis chase Bond (ROGER MOORE), who skis off an enormous cliff in the Austrian Alps (actually Mt. Asgaard in northern Canada). He falls for what seems like an eternity, then pulls a ripcord that releases a parachute. The tension of this sequence is heightened by the use of widescreen in capturing a tiny image of Bond (stuntman Ric Sylvester) skiing towards the vast edge of Mt. Asgaard. This really was a fantastic stunt that left the Bond producers with the arduous task of trying to top it.

3. *Bond's midair parachute theft in Moonraker*

In *The Spy Who Loved Me*, Bond (ROGER MOORE) has a parachute to save him when he skis off a mountain cliff. How do you attempt to top that? In the pre-title sequence of *Moonraker*, the producers drop him from a similar height—without the parachute! Bond is on a plane with a villain who shoots out the plane's controls and then jumps out, with a parachute safely strapped to his back. While Bond is watching him fall, the villainous Jaws (RICHARD KIEL) pushes him out sans parachute. Bond is falling steadily and sees that the man who jumped before him hasn't yet pulled his ripcord. Arching his back into his best sky-diving position, Bond literally flies through the air until he slams into the man and they start an epic battle in midair for control of the man's parachute. Of course, Bond wrests the parachute away and secures it to himself as the man drops to his death. A stunt that is the epitome of "high flying."

4. Bond hanging from the plane in Octopussy

Towards the climax of the movie, Octopussy (MAUD ADAMS) has been captured by villain Kamal Khan (LOUIS

Bond (ROGER MOORE) hangs on in Octopussy

JOURDAN) and his henchman Gobinda (KABIR BEDI) and put
on board Kamal's plane. It is heading down the runway for
take off, when 007 (ROGER MOORE) gallops up behind the
plane on horseback. Bond leaps from the horse onto the
tail of the plane as it lifts off. The plane soars into the air
with Bond spread-eagled on top of the fuselage. Kamal
knows that he is there and puts the plane into a 360-degree
spin but incredibly Bond hangs on. Bond edges to the
wing of the plane and begins pulling the wiring out of one
of the engines. "He'll kill us all!" a panicked Kamal
laments. "Go out and get him," he orders Gobinda. "Out
there?" a shocked Gobinda replies. "Go!" says Kamal
sternly. "Yes, Excellency," says a dutiful and very hesitant
Gobinda. Gobinda clambers out the side of the plane and
onto the fuselage to battle Bond. The battle ends with
Bond flicking the plane's antenna into Gobinda's face,
which destabilizes him and sends him hurtling to his
death.

5. Bond bungee jumping from the dam in GoldenEye

Bond (PIERCE BROSNAN) needs to get in to a secret chemical weapons plant in the Soviet Union. Its entrance is at the
base of a huge dam with steep walls. 007 has thought of a
novel way of getting to the plant: bungee jumping. He runs
across the top of the dam, ties his bungee cord to the top of
it, steps to the edge and dives off. He drops gracefully down
the dam wall and fires a piton-gun into the top of the

weapons plant, which he will soon destroy. I wonder if this jump earned him a 10.0 from the Russian judge?

Military Battles

James Bond films usually end with a bang, literally and figuratively. But before that bang can occur, the good guys (U.S. Army, British Royal Navy, Japanese Ninjas, Greek smugglers, circus acrobats, Afghan rebels, etc.), who are assisting Bond, and the villains' loyal supporters have to engage in a really big battle. Machine guns, grenades, explosions, noise, in fact, total mayhem, it's all part of the fun. Of all the "military" battles the five best are:

1. Thunderball

Every time I watch the climactic underwater battle in *Thunderball*, I ask myself, as I'm sure others do: "How the hell did they ever film this?" What did it take to coordinate and film about 40 divers, sea-cruisers, sharks and spear guns underwater? The result, while a little long, is exhilarating. Orange wet-suit clad U.S. Marine Aqua-paras (the good guys) battle SPECTRE's black wet-suited frogmen (the bad guys) in a battle to the death with knives and spear-guns. Things aren't going too well for the good guys until Bond (SEAN CONNERY) arrives with a gadget-laden jet pack attached to his back. It's rather bloody for a Bond film, but great cinema.

2. The Spy Who Loved Me

Almost nothing beats the military battle finale of *The Spy Who Loved Me*; it is Bondian mayhem at its best. Captured British and American submariners have been held aboard the submarine-swallowing oil tanker, the Liparus, owned by the evil Stromberg (CURT JUERGENS). With Bond (ROGER MOORE) in the lead, they break out. What follows is a well-choreographed ballet of machine guns, grenades, explosions, and general chaos, which includes 007 disarming a live nuclear missile in one of the most tense moments of the series.

Did you know that?

The American military aids James Bond in five "military" battles: *Goldfinger*; *Thunderball*; *Diamonds Are Forever*; *The Spy Who Loved Me*; *Moonraker*.

Bond (SEAN CONNERY) leads the chase in You Only Live Twice

3. You Only Live Twice

This film's military battle adds the word "epic" to the series, although the star of the sequence is the set—Blofeld's massive volcano hideout. Bond (SEAN CONNERY) and the Ninjas of the Japanese Secret Service combat Blofeld's cohorts in a battle royal that show the samurai wielding Ninjas at their deadly best. And 007 and Blofeld (DONALD PLEASENCE) come face to face for the first time. When Bond is revealed to him, Blofeld says, "James Bond. They told me you were assassinated in Hong Kong." "Yes," Bond replies. "This is my second life." "You Only Live Twice, Mr. Bond," Blofeld retorts.

Bond (GEORGE LAZENBY) readies to fire
in On Her Majesty's Secret Service

4. *On Her Majesty's Secret Service*

Blofeld has another mountain hideout, Piz Gloria, this one nestled in the beautiful Swiss Alps, where Bond's fiancée Tracy (DIANA RIGG) is being held prisoner. Bond (GEORGE LAZENBY), aided by Marc-Ange Draco (GABRIELE FERZETTI), his fiancée's father and head of an organized crime syndicate, arrive via helicopter with Draco's men to rescue Tracy and kill Blofeld (TELLY SAVALAS). It is a thrilling helicopter attack, expertly filmed amidst the Alpine backdrop, with the tension mounting during the battle and as Tracy is rescued; but Blofeld escapes. Probably the best moment is when an elderly scientist in Blofeld's laboratory hurls a flask filled with some sort of toxic chemical at 007. Bond ducks at the last moment and the flask smashes into the wall, causing a large piece of it to disintegrate. Bond fires his machine gun and kills the scientist; and then does a priceless double-take when he sees the gaping hole in the wall left by the flask.

5. *Moonraker*

Most of the action in *Moonraker* is of the slapstick variety and the military battle at the end is no exception. It is still stunning, however, to watch troops of American astronauts (aided immensely by John Barry's haunting music) floating out into space from their space shuttle and battling Drax' men. The laser beams flying away are actually reminiscent of the underwater battle in *Thunderball*, with the lasers taking the place of spear guns, and making the special effects here as good as anything in the *Star Wars* series.

One-On-One Fights

While many action films have fight sequences involving plenty of fists flailing about indiscriminately, a Bond fight has a careful choreography of fists, kicks, judo chops and broken furniture, shot in such a way that the audience can follow in detail every crash and blow. That Bond never seems to get bloodied or bruised in these skirmishes doesn't diminish their entertainment value. These are Bond films we're talking about, not Scorsese gangster flicks! Here are the five best one-on-one fights:

1. Bond vs. Red Grant in From Russia With Love

007 (SEAN CONNERY) and SPECTRE assassin Red Grant (ROBERT SHAW) fight on board the Orient Express in what is generally considered one of the greatest fights in film history. Its greatness coming because it isn't merely a fight between two men, rather it is a *fight-to-the-death* between two men. There is a viciousness as both men struggle tenaciously within the small train compartment that is rarely seen on film. The scene's impact is heightened by the absence of music on the soundtrack while the fight is taking place. We hear all the brutal grunts and groans of the combatants and

the steady churning of the moving train in the background. When at last Bond overpowers Grant and strangles him with his own garrote, it is almost a relief that this intense struggle is over.

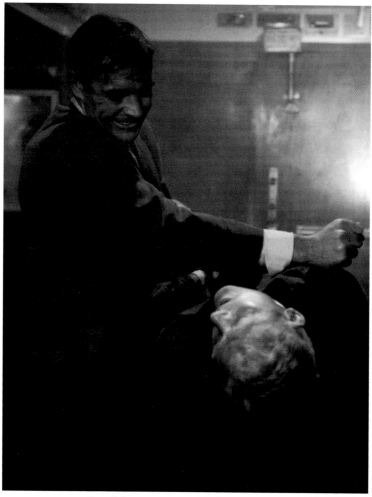

Bond (SEAN CONNERY) belts Red Grant (ROBERT SHAW)
in From Russia With Love

Did you know that?

Drugs have rendered 007 unconscious 6 times: drugged coffee in *Dr. No*; tranquilizer gun in *Goldfinger*; gas blown into the penthouse elevator of the Whyte House in Las Vegas in *Diamonds Are Forever*; "cigarette" smoke in *The Spy Who Loved Me*; chloral hydrate laced vodka martini in *The Living Daylights*; tranquilizer dart fired into his neck in *GoldenEye*.

2. Bond vs. Capungo in Goldfinger

Bond (SEAN CONNERY) fights with Capungo (ALF JOINT) in the pretitle sequence of *Goldfinger*. Bond's lady-friend has just stepped out of the tub and started to kiss him when she opens her eyes and sees Capungo come out from behind a dresser, with a club in his hand. Bond senses the girl's distraction and pulls away. As he does, he sees the reflection of Capungo in the girl's eyes! Capungo raises the club behind Bond, who spins the girl around so that she gets hit. 007 and Capungo fight, trading punches, body-flips and broken furniture until, after a fast and furious scrap, Bond flings the man into the bathtub. Capungo reaches for Bond's Walther PPK which is hanging in its holster near the tub. He grabs the gun, just as Bond notices a plugged-in electric heater sitting on the table next to him. Capungo readies to fire. Bond knocks the heater into the tub, and Capungo is instantly electrocuted. A shocking conclusion to a great fight!

3. Bond vs. Osato's henchman in You Only Live Twice

Of all the choreographed one-on-one fights of the series, the battle between 007 (SEAN CONNERY) and Osato's hulking henchman in *You Only Live Twice* is the best. In the penthouse office of Mr. Osato, Bond's heavy-set attacker flings him about and 007 fends him off with an office couch, to no avail. He even dodges three swipes from a samurai sword before using a well-timed body-flip and a stone sculpture (slammed across the man's back) to knock his assailant out cold. A great example of the Bond team's genius at staging entertaining and suspenseful fight sequences.

4. Bond vs. Sandor in The Spy Who Loved Me

Staged on a rooftop in Cairo, the confrontation here is between Bond (ROGER MOORE) and Stromberg henchman Sandor (MILTON REID), a man who seemingly has no neck and a body like a tank. But against his larger foe 007 more than holds his own as the two men trade punches, kicks, judo chops and bearhugs. Eventually the struggle brings both men near the edge of the rooftop. Bond lands a punch that appears to send Sandor over the edge, but he grabs hold of Bond's tie as he totters over the edge. His grip is loosening as

Bond asks him, "Where's Fekkesh?" "Pyramids," the desperate Sandor replies. Bond swats at the tongue of his tie, and sends Sandor to his death. "What a helpful chap," Bond comments as he straightens his tie.

5. Bond vs. Peter Franks in Diamonds Are Forever

A small elevator might be the last place you'd think you'd expect to find an entertaining fight, and yet that is exactly where 007 (SEAN CONNERY) and diamond smuggler Peter Franks (JOE ROBINSON) engage in one. Though lacking the drama of Bond's fight with Red Grant in *From Russia With Love*, some of the same viciousness and fight-to-the-death qualities are evident. Featured are fists, broken glass and, when the struggle spills out of the elevator and into the hall-

Did you know that?

James Bond has battled bad guys inside or on top of a train five times: *From Russia With Love* (vs. Red Grant); *Live and Let Die* (vs. Tee Hee); *The Spy Who Loved Me* (vs. Jaws) *Octopussy* (vs. Gobinda and Grischka); *GoldenEye* (vs. Trevelyan, Xenia and General Ouromov)

way, a fire extinguisher that Bond uses to disorient Franks, before kicking him down the stairs to his death.

Honorable mention: Bond vs. Jacques Boivard in *Thunderball*; Bond vs. Jaws on the train in *The Spy Who Loved Me*; Bond vs. Trevelyan in *GoldenEye*.

Shootouts

Bond films are noted for their exceptional gun-play. Pit Bond and his Walther PPK (or any other gun that he happens to get his hands on) against a few baddies, and a rewarding action sequence is usually at hand. The five most notable shootouts are:

1. For Your Eyes Only

Bond (ROGER MOORE) joins Greek smuggler Columbo (TOPOL) and his band of merry men to attack villain Kristatos' seaport warehouse in Albania. Bond and the men sneak into the port by boat and with some good aim shoot their way into the warehouse, as well as using some fists and knives to overcome the bad guys. The fine orchestration of the sequence makes it a standout amongst shootouts.

2. Octopussy

007 (ROGER MOORE) chases the evil Soviet General Orlov (STEPHEN BERKOFF) from a stationary train. However, waiting outside of the train are several machine-gun-toting Soviet soldiers. As General Orlov runs by, he shouts to the soldiers, "Kill him! Kill him!" The soldiers start firing on Bond, who ducks behind the train. His return fire from his Walther takes out the soldiers and frees Bond to continue chasing Orlov.

Bond (ROGER MOORE) takes aim in Octopussy

Director John Glen's expert filming gives tension to a short sequence.

3. From Russia With Love

James Bond (SEAN CONNERY) and Kerim Bey (PEDRO AR-MENDARIZ) are invited guests at a gypsy camp outside Istanbul. A band of Bulgarians led by KGB sympathizer Krilencu attack suddenly and mayhem ensues. Using his Walther Bond lends his assistance and eliminates as many of the attackers as he can which earns him the respect of his gypsy hosts. This sequence is the first in the series to feature 007 using his gun to such deadly effect.

4. A View To A Kill

Hardly has James Bond (ROGER MOORE) sneaked into Stacy Sutton's house to question her, when the house is attacked by several of Max Zorin's thugs. Bond grabs the shotgun that Stacy (TANYA ROBERTS) had been pointing at him and goes to work on the bad guys. He blasts several guys at near point-blank range and knocks them down, but after a few moments, they get up and continue the attack. "What's this loaded with?" Bond questions Stacy as he checks the weapon. "Rock salt," she replies. "Now you tell me," he exclaims. Despite the impressive effect caused by the shotgun, 007 tosses it aside and continues the fight the old-fashioned way, with his fists. A good shootout in an otherwise uninspired film.

An AK-47 protects Bond (PIERCE BROSNAN) and
Natalya (ISABELLA SCORUPCO) in GoldenEye

Did you know that?

James Bond has fired a machine gun on the bad guys in seven films: *On Her Majesty's Secret Service* (the "military" battle at Piz Gloria); *The Spy Who Loved Me* (the "military" battle on the Liparus); *Octopussy* (sliding down the banister at the Monsoon Palace); *The Living Daylights* (on board a Soviet transport plane in Afghanistan); *GoldenEye* (the pretitle sequence in Russia; escaping a St. Petersburg prison; firing at Xenia's helicopter in the Cuban jungle; chasing Trevelyan on top of the GoldenEye antenna); *Tomorrow Never Dies* (the teaser at the Khyber Pass; escaping from Carver's office in Saigon; onboard Carver's stealth ship); *The World Is Not Enough* (pursuing Renard and his men in the underground nuclear warhead storage facility).

5. *Tomorrow Never Dies*

The finale of *Tomorrow Never Dies* presents one of the better shootouts among the many in the Brosnan Bond films. 007 (PIERCE BROSNAN) and Chinese agent Wai Lin (MICHELLE YEOH) infiltrate maniacal Elliot Carver's stealth ship. Before long all hell breaks loose. Using every machine gun and pistol that they can lay their hands on, Bond and his Chinese partner blast away Carver's minions. Though some-

thing of overkill, their success foils Carver's plans to start a
war between China and Great Britain. From the viewers
point of view it works better than a similar sequence in

007 (PIERCE BROSNAN) loads up in Tomorrow Never Dies

GoldenEye, where Bond shoots his way out of a Russian prison cell.

Explosions

Bond movies live by the big-bang theory: the bigger the explosion, the more the audience likes it. With explosions used in movies more frequently these days, the Bond movie detonations are less exciting than they used to be, but a few stand out. I still like the following five:

1. The exploding boats in *From Russia With Love*

Bond (SEAN CONNERY) and Tatiana (DANIELA BIANCHI) are escaping across the northern Adriatic Sea in a fast speedboat when a flotilla of SPECTRE boats attack, using machine guns and grenades. The bullets puncture several fuel drums in Bond's boat and the fuel leaks out. Is Bond's luck at an end? Bond releases the drums and they fall into the sea, still spilling fuel. Bond slows the boat and puts his hands up in surrender. Intent on capturing Bond, the boats close in and pull alongside the fuel drums. 007 picks up a flare gun and fires two shots in the direction of the drums. The fuel ignites in a mass of fireballs of inferno proportions that destroy the SPECTRE boats.

2. *The landing craft in Live and Let Die*

Bond (ROGER MOORE) has eluded a bevy of bad guys and the Louisiana State Police by racing his speedboat through some of Louisiana's twisting bayous. Only one pursuer is left, a Dr. Kananga henchman, who in his own speedboat chases Bond to a deadend. Bond races back toward his pursuer and as their boats pass, flings some gasoline from a canister at the man which hits him and blinds him. Seizing this opportunity, 007 brings his boat alongside his pursuer's and directs the latter's at full speed towards the open end of a large, abandoned WWII landing craft moored in the bayou. Bond pulls away as the henchman's boat races up the ramp and into the craft, where it crashes into the back and causes what may be the biggest and brightest explosion in the Bond films—maybe in any film.

3. *The Disco Volante in Thunderball*

Domino (CLAUDINE AUGER) has killed baddie Emilio Largo and rescued 007 (SEAN CONNERY). But they have one prob-

Did you know that?

For Your Eyes Only is the only film in the series not to feature an explosion at or near the end of the movie.

lem: Largo's body has jammed the controls of the boat they are on, the Disco Volante. And the Disco Volante (Flying Saucer) is living up to its name and racing through the water at a perilous speed. Bond and Domino realize that the boat will soon hit one of the islands they are passing and they jump into the water at the last minute. The Disco Volante slams into an island and is literally blown sky-high. The explosion is particularly impressive because the boat virtually disintegrates on impact and only flotsam and a fortunate Bond and Domino are left in its wake.

4. The tanker truck in Licence To Kill

Bond (TIMOTHY DALTON) and drug lord Franz Sanchez (ROBERT DAVI) have just rolled over down the side of a hill on top of an oil-tanker truck. Bond is battered and struggles to get to his feet, but he is stopped by a machete-wielding Sanchez, who is drenched in gasoline from the now leaking tanker that lays on it side beside them. Sanchez raises the machete, poised to slice Bond in two. Sanchez has found out that Bond, who he thought was his ally, is really his enemy. "Don't you want to know why?" Bond asks wearily as he pulls a lighter out of his pocket. He shows Sanchez the lighter's inscription, "To James, love Della and Felix." Sanchez had had Della murdered and Felix, Bond's best friend, maimed. Bond was the best man at their wedding. Realization hits home for Sanchez. Bond flicks the lighter, whose extra-long flame shoots up and catches Sanchez' gasoline-drenched clothes, turning him into a human fireball. Sanchez' fiery body sets off the gasoline that has leaked from the tanker truck, until the vehicle explodes violently and is engulfed in bright orange flames. We can scarcely believe the amazing shot of Bond running away from this conflagration.

Bond (TIMOTHY DALTON) is nearly roasted in Licence To Kill

5. *The cruise missile in Tomorrow Never Dies*

A British cruise missile heads towards a terrorist arms bazaar in Afghanistan. 007 (PIERCE BROSNAN) is on the ground, at the bazaar, where there is a stolen Russian jet that happens to have nuclear cruise missiles strapped to its wings. Bond must shoot his way out of the bazaar. He decides to get the jet in the air before the British missile hits. Hardly has Bond lifted off, than the cruise missile hits. The explosion it causes is so big it fills the entire screen with orange flame. But where is Bond? Did the jet escape the devastation? The explosion is billowing in all its glory, when Bond's jet shoots through the middle it, moving so fast that the flames do 007 and the jet no harm.

Helicopter Explosions

For as long as I can remember I have been afraid of helicopters, and have sworn never to step foot in one. Searching for a reason for my fear, I realized it stemmed directly from my exposure to the James Bond films. Because whenever a helicopter appears in a James Bond movie, there is a good chance that it will soon explode into a bright orange fireball. The five best explosions of helicopters are:

1. *A View To A Kill*

The teaser has James Bond (ROGER MOORE) firing a flare at the Soviet helicopter that is pursuing him. The flare enters the cockpit and sprays red smoke everywhere, which disorients the pilot and he loses control. The copter crashes into the side of an iceberg. You can hear the metal screech when it hits. The memory of the bright orange fireball against the backdrop of huge shiny white icebergs is not easily forgotten.

2. *GoldenEye*

007 (PIERCE BROSNAN) and Natalya (ISABELLA SCORUPCO) have been strapped down in a stolen Tiger helicopter which the bad guys have programmed to fire air-to-air missiles *at itself*. As the missiles launch outward, Bond tries desperately to release himself from the restraining straps. The missiles turn back towards the copter and close in. Bond sees a way out—the ejector seat button, and slams his head against it. He and Natalya in the passenger carriage shoot upwards just as the missiles reach their target. The resulting explosion is so large—probably the biggest helicopter explosion of the series—that the fireball almost reaches the passenger carriage as it thrusts skyward.

3. *Diamonds Are Forever*

Mr. Wint (BRUCE GLOVER) and Mr. Kidd (PUTTER SMITH) hand over a box to a couple of diamond smugglers who have landed a small helicopter in the South African desert. The smugglers think that the box contains diamonds, whereas Wint and Kidd have put in explosives. Shortly after the smugglers lift off, the chopper explodes and just about disintegrates. "Funny," says Mr. Wint, "how everyone who touches those diamonds seems to...die."

4. You Only Live Twice

Bond (SEAN CONNERY) is flying over the Japanese countryside in "Little Nellie," his one-man autogyro helicopter, when four conventional helicopters attack him, all equipped with machine guns. But they don't stand a chance. Bond's copter is equipped with a wide array of defense mechanisms which he uses in rapid succession to send the four copters to a hot, explosive death. A flame thrower, aerial mines, rockets, and air-to-air missiles add four helicopter explosions to the series' scorecard.

5. From Russia With Love

Nearing the movie's end Bond (SEAN CONNERY) is escaping across moorland, pursued by a SPECTRE helicopter. Its occupants are hurling grenades at Bond as they maneuver. But Bond pulls a small rifle from his attache' case and aims at the copter. Before one of the occupants can throw another grenade, 007 fires up at him and hits the man in the arm. The man drops the grenade to the floor of the copter, and it explodes. This helicopter explosion proved to be the first of many for the series.

Academy-Award–winning composer John Barry

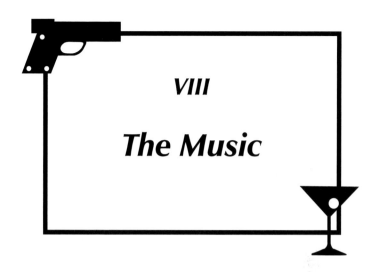

VIII

The Music

James Bond music has a style all its own: The scores and songs are lush, loud, and full of bombast, and all just a little over the top. It's a prefect style for the Bond films, making the music an integral part of the series' formula. As well as highlighting the best scores and songs, this section pokes some fun at the worst songs.

Musical Scores

Listening to Oscar winner John Barry's majestic Bond film scores has always made me feel they were way too serious for

Did you know that?

Marvin Hamlisch's score for *The Spy Who Loved Me* is the only Bond score to be nominated for an Oscar.

the subject matter. But that's a main reason they are so effective. The sometimes beautiful, sometimes foreboding scores lend reality to these fantasy films that for the moment allow an audience to believe that the end of the world may be near and could happen if Bond doesn't save the day. Any good fantasy needs such a touch of realism to make it fulfilling. Barry, who scored eleven Bond films (including six of the first seven), created the classic Bond sound which his successors have had a tough time following. His successors include Marvin Hamlisch, who provided a unique sound for *The Spy Who Loved Me*, and George Martin, Bill Conti, Michael Kamen, Eric Serra, and David Arnold, with only Hamlisch and Arnold producing scores worthy of a Bond film. The most effective scores are all by John Barry, except one:

1. On Her Majesty's Secret Service

This score works on every level: it captures and enhances the film's varying moments of excitement, romance, love, and tragedy. Perhaps the prettiest and most atmospheric tune of the series is the one which accompanies Bond being escorted via helicopter through the Swiss Alps to Blofeld's mountain retreat, "Journey to Blofeld's Hideaway."

2. You Only Live Twice

To add local color, Barry perfectly blended the classic Bondian sound with traditional Japanese music, while never letting you forget that this is a Bond film. "Mountains and Sunsets," played while Bond and Kissy row up the bay in search of Blofeld's volcano, never fails to give me chills.

3. Goldfinger

Both title song and score for this film are big, bold and brassy. It's a daring sound that permeates the film's every moment and sets the tone for all future Bond scores.

4. Moonraker

John Barry displays all of his talents in composing such grand and majestic music for the space scenes. For the South American rainforest scenes the music is lyrical and sweeping. For Corrine being fed to the dogs it is threatening and scary. It is a joy to listen to the whole range of Bondian musical styles in one movie. (Listen to Barry's Oscar-winning score for *Out of Africa*—written six years later—and you will hear marked similarities to his *Moonraker* score.)

5. The World Is Not Enough

Better than choose another John Barry score, which are all so good, I wish to acknowledge David Arnold. He is the only composer who has come close to nailing down the Bond sound and hit his stride with his second Bond score, *The World Is Not Enough*, after a fine first try with *Tomorrow Never Dies*. Using variations of the classic Bond theme, Arnold combines the sweeping and lyrical Barry sound with a modern techno sound that feels like Bond.

Honorable mention: *Thunderball; Diamonds Are Forever; Tomorrow Never Dies.*

Best Songs

Not your normal pop song, a Bond theme song is a unique animal. It features music that is definitely over the top, and has sometimes downright cheesy lyrics. But what fun they are to listen to. Although popular music style has changed in 40 years, Bond songs have stayed refreshingly the same! And the five best are:

1. "Live And Let Die," Paul McCartney and Wings

McCartney and Wings may seem like an odd choice to perform a Bond song, but 29 years after its release it remains

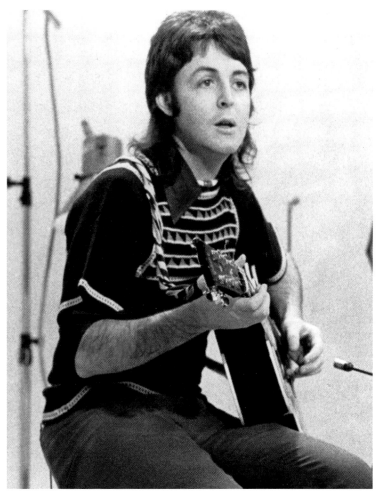

Paul McCartney

the best, as well as one of McCartney's best post-Beatles songs. The midsection instrumental is repeated to great effect during the film's famous boat chase.

2. *"Goldfinger,"*
Shirley Bassey

The quintessential Bond song from the quintessential Bond movie—big, bold and brassy. Bassey's style set the tone for Bond theme songs. In fact several later Bond songs are obviously thinly veiled copies of this classic. (Think *Licence To Kill* or *GoldenEye*.)

3. *"Nobody Does It Better"*
(The Spy Who Loved Me),
Carly Simon

Set to a great melody, this song's lyrics truly define Bond's character, "Nobody does it better, /makes me feel sad for the rest, /nobody does it half as good as you, /baby you're the best."

4. *"For Your Eyes Only,"*
Sheena Easton

One of the prettiest Bond songs, this song helped make Sheena Easton a star in the early 80s. The melody is also put to good use in the scenic Greek location scenes in the film, enhancing the romantic mood of the Greek isles.

Duran Duran

5. "A View To A Kill," Duran Duran

Bond veteran John Barry collaborated with 80s pop chart toppers Duran Duran on this high-energy, hard-rocking song. Aside from its use in the movie, the song reached #1 on the U.S. Pop Charts—a first for a Bond song. The song with accompanying video appeared on MTV—another Bond first.

Honorable mention: "Thunderball"—Tom Jones; "Diamonds Are Forever"—Shirley Bassey; "Where Are You?" (theme from *Moonraker*)—Shirley Bassey.

Worst Songs

Here are the five worst:

1. *"The Experience of Love"*
(endtitle song from GoldenEye),
Eric Serra

The melody and tempo of the song are completely inappropriate for a Bond film. Eric Serra, who composed the awful score for the film, also wrote and sang this real downer of a song that plays during the end-credits of the film. His voice sounds like a dying animal. It's no way to end Bond film!

2. *"The Living Daylights,"*
A-ha

A-ha, one-hit wonders from the Netherlands, were chosen by the Bond producers based on the success of their 1986 hit video, "Take On Me." My first reaction to this drab song was "uh-oh," and it ended their international popularity.

3. *"From Russia With Love,"* Matt Munro

It's not that crooner Matt Munro's song is bad, it's just not what we've come to know as a Bond song. It's more 50s style ballad than bombastic and sexual Bond song. It became a dated relic as soon as "Goldfinger" came out a year later in 1964.

4. *"All Time High,"* (from Octopussy), Rita Coolidge

Rita Coolidge was not the right choice to sing this song written by John Barry. The melody and music are not bad, but the song cries out for someone with a little more sass (Shirley Bassey perhaps?). Coolidge never lifts the song to the "All Time High" that the song promises.

5. *"Tomorrow Never Dies,"* Sheryl Crow

Another instance of a Bond song not hitting the mark. I like Sheryl Crow a lot, but this is too much of a kitschy lounge act. Crow's bluesy/folksy voice accompanied by twangy guitars lacks the excitement and verve needed for a Bond song. The end-title song, "Surrender" by K.D. Lang, is much better and would have been more appropriate as the opening song.

Mr. Wint (BRUCE GLOVER) goes for the kill against Bond (SEAN CONNERY) in Diamonds Are Forever

IX

Miscellaneous Encounters

To cover areas that although mainstays of the films, don't fit neatly into the book's previous categories, I've added this section. Enjoy.

Worst Moments

It's obvious that I love James Bond films. But, as much as I love them, I have to concede that there are moments in the series that are bad, even embarrassing. But, hey, after 40 years and 19 films, not every moment is going to be a gem, right? The five worst moments are:

1. *"California Girls" in A View To A Kill*

The pretitle sequence has James Bond (ROGER MOORE) riding a snowmobile across the Siberian ice chased by a Soviet helicopter and Soviet ski-troops. Bond is sent flying off his

Bond (ROGER MOORE) snowboards in A View To A Kill

snowmobile by sudden cannon fire from the copter. The snowmobile explodes in a ball of fire. The ski troops near their foe, when Bond catches a break. A ski from his destroyed snowmobile has landed intact, right beside him. He hops on it and starts snow surfing down an incline. So far, so good. The moment is completely ruined by the soundtrack—the Beach Boys singing "California Girls"—an awful attempt at silly humor. An exciting chase turns a James Bond movie into a Jerry Lewis movie. Without a doubt, the lowest point of the entire series.

2. Jaws and girlfriend in Moonraker

Moonraker has many downright silly moments, but none worse than when Jaws (RICHARD KIEL) meets the love of his life. After having failed to kill 007 once again, supposedly evil henchman Jaws is riding in a speeding cable-car. It crashes into the car docking area and turns the entire place into a pile of rubble. Jaws miraculously digs himself out and comes face to face with a petite, young woman, with ridiculous Goldilocks' hair. She hands him a flower and they fall instantly in love (while some overly-romantic music plays on the soundtrack). Even writing this, I can't believe the scene I describe actually happened in a James Bond movie.

3. J.W. Pepper and the elephant in The Man with the Golden Gun

We had been amused by Sheriff J.W. Pepper (CLIFTON JAMES) in *Live And Let Die,* where his appearance stopped just short of going over the top. His return in the subsequent film, *The Man with the Golden Gun,* isn't as amusing. Pepper, has been watching 007 escape in a speed boat along a Thai canal, chased by Hai Fat's henchmen. Pepper turns aside, sees a young elephant standing next to him and says to the animal, "Boy, you is ugly." The elephant lurches up and knocks Pepper headfirst into the canal. This sequence has nothing to do with the rest of the film and nothing to do with James Bond.

4. The gondola in Venice's Piazza San Marco in Moonraker

The entire gondola chase through the canals of Venice is stupid. But, just when you think the stupidity is over, it gets worse. Bond (ROGER MOORE) eludes the bad guys using a souped-up gondola. Activating one of its many gadgets, he flips a switch that inflates the bottom of the gondola and it climbs out of the canal right into the middle of the Piazza San Marco. Bond then drives the gondola-car through the square watched by a befuddled crowd. Again, in a Jerry Lewis movie, this sequence would be funny but in a Bond movie it is plain idiotic.

5. The Tarzan yell in Octopussy

For the most part, *Octopussy* is a good Bond movie that plays it straight, but has one moment that makes you cringe. Bond (ROGER MOORE) has escaped from Kamal Khan's Indian fortress and is trudging through the jungle pursued hotly by

Kamal and his men. At one point, Bond grabs a long vine and swings through the trees a la Tarzan. This would be an effective moment if the producers hadn't felt it necessary to accompany it with an authentic Tarzan yell over the soundtrack. A bad attempt at a cheap laugh.

Animal Adventures

Aside from dodging gun-toting baddies and henchmen with steel teeth and deadly bowler hats, 007 has also had to deal with mortal threats from the animal kingdom. Whether it be sharks, piranhas, maggots, alligators, snakes, tarantulas, electric eels or tigers, our smaller-brained brethren have not always been kind to Mr. Bond. Of all such encounters the five most interesting are:

1. Alligators in Live and Let Die

James Bond (ROGER MOORE) has been captured and taken to an alligator farm in Louisiana. He is left on a shallow bayou swarming with gators and crocs. The gators come closer and it seems that Bond has no way out. Until he notices that the backs of four gators sitting in the water a few feet apart from each other make a bridge to the land that Bond needs to reach. So he leaps one foot first onto the back of the first creature and "hop-scotches" across the backs of the next three and onto land and safety. This has to be the fanciest footwork of Bond's career.

2. The tarantula in Dr. No

Suddenly James Bond (SEAN CONNERY) wakes from a peaceful sleep in his Jamaican hotel room and discovers a tarantula crawling on him. Afraid that any movement on his part might cause the spider to sting him, a nervous 007 sits completely still as the tarantula slowly walks up his arm. Finally it crawls off his arm and Bond knocks it off the bed, grabs a shoe and slams the creature repeatedly until he kills it. Perhaps Q should have given him a watch that turned into a can of insect repellent!

3. Maggots in Licence To Kill

The maggots Bond (TIMOTHY DALTON) finds in the aquarium of drug runner Milton Krest in *Licence To Kill* don't pose any threat to him, but they do help him out of a precarious situation. Having sneaked into the aquarium, 007 inspects the various fish tanks, before he spots some strange metallic drawers. He pushes a button and a drawer slides open. It is filled with maggots. Bond is suspicious, so he rolls up his sleeves, buries his hands in the mess and finds bags of cocaine hidden under the maggots. With his hands still in the maggots, Bond feels a security guard's gun to his head. "Hold it," the guard says. "Do you mind if I get my hands out of here?" asks Bond. "Sure, do it slowly," the guard replies. As

007 (TIMOTHY DALTON) gets a handful of maggots in Licence To Kill

he lifts his hands free, Bond grasps a fistful of maggots, turns slowly around, and flings them in the guard's face. The man is thrown off-guard which allows Bond to punch him and flip him into the drawer, right on top of the maggots. Bond pushes the button again and the drawer slides closed with the guard trapped inside. A win-win situation for Bond and the maggots!

Did you know that?

James Bond has had ominous encounters with snakes on 3 occasions: *Live and Let Die* (in his hotel room in San Monique); *Moonraker* (in a pool in Drax' South American hideout); *Octopussy* (while lying in the Indian jungle outside Khan's fortress).

A boa gets a crush on Bond (ROGER MOORE) in Moonraker

4. The tiger in Octopussy

Kamal Khan and his baddies are pursuing 007 through the jungle. Throughout the chase, Bond (ROGER MOORE) is set upon by alligators and leeches, but, when he thinks it can't get any worse, a large Bengal tiger steps in front of him. To let Bond know that he is not welcome, the tiger roars furiously, which puts Bond at a loss at what to do. Suprisingly, he raises his hand and in his best animal-trainer voice commands, "Sit!" The tiger obeys, allowing Bond to escape. Implausible, you think? You mean you don't believe the great 007's voice has the charisma enough to make a tiger sit?

5. *Sharks in Thunderball*

Bond (SEAN CONNERY) is spying in the Bahamian home of villain Emilio Largo (ADOLFO CELI), when Largo's guards spot him. As he is trying to escape from the grounds, one of the men jumps him and they both fall into the pool. Largo and his henchmen arrive on the scene, but he decides against shooting Bond (will Bond villains ever learn?) in the pool; he has "a better idea." A lever he pulls on the side of the pool releases a metal curtain that slides over the top of the pool and covers it. Bond and his assailant are trapped. A hatch to an adjoining pool opens and, you guessed it, some very large and very hungry Golden Grotto sharks pour through it toward the still fighting pair. In the nick of time, Bond stabs his attacker, whose blood clouds the water so the sharks have something to chase other than Bond. One shark after another swim past him toward the bleeding man and Bond sneaks through the hatch into the other pool and to safety. A stray shark swims at him as he climbs out, but the shark is too late. "Sorry old boy. Better luck next time," says Bond.

Main Titles

A Bond movie wouldn't be a Bond movie without the main-title sequence, when after the pretitle sequence, the opening credits roll and the theme song plays. Generally it is a collage of psychedelic images of silhouetted nude women and phallic symbols, against an eye-dazzling array of colors. That today's Bond films continue the tradition of this dated, 60s symbolism, testifies to and celebrates their importance to the Bond formula. I mean, we're talking James Bond movies here. What kind of James Bond movie would it be without naked women and phallic symbols prancing around during the main-titles? The five best are:

1. Thunderball

This film's main title sequence is so good that all of the Bond films since seem to imitate it. For the first time we saw silhouetted bodies of naked women floating across the screen, being pursued by phallic symbols (in this case, spearguns in the hands of frogmen). These erotic images, coupled with the pulsating theme song by Tom Jones, set the tone perfectly for the film.

2. *GoldenEye*

The cold war was over, the Berlin wall was down and the Soviet Union had collapsed by 1995 when *GoldenEye* was released. Six years had passed since the previous 007 film and much in the world had changed. *GoldenEye*'s main title takes great advantage of these events. Yes, the nude women remain, but this staple is now accompanied by fantastic images of statues of Lenin crumbling and hammers and sickles falling. And woven through it all are images of Bond's Walther PPK. Together they drive home the point: The cold war may be over and the Soviet Union gone, but James Bond is alive and kicking.

3. *The Spy Who Loved Me*

In another first, this main title has naked women prancing around Bond himself rather than phallic symbols. Roger Moore's Bond runs around the screen, gun in hand, while the women dance around him. The remaining Roger Moore films and the two Timothy Dalton films repeated this approach.

4. *Live and Let Die*

Although not a very imaginative main-title, it contains one memorable and lasting image. A voodoo high priestess stares into frame, and just as Paul McCartney sings, "Say live and let die," her head turns into a skull with bright red flames shooting from it. This motif continues throughout the main title and, combined with the powerful McCartney song, makes it one of the best.

5. For Your Eyes Only

A twist was added to all of the standard main-title elements: it features Sheena Easton singing the Oscar nominated title song. Looking very much the Bond girl herself, Easton's image intertwines with the nude silhouettes to create a unique sequence that pleases the eyes and ears.

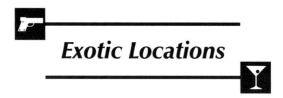

Exotic Locations

There are few places on earth that 007 hasn't traveled to over the course of 19 movies, many of them exotic. While some are locations you might think twice about traveling to (Afghanistan and Azerbaijan to name a couple), most are quite breathtaking. The following are the five best:

1. The island of Phuket in The Man with the Golden Gun

The island of Phuket off the coast of Thailand is without a doubt the most stunning location in the entire Bond series.

Bond (ROGER MOORE) and Goodnight (BRIT EKLAND) escape Scaramanga's island in The Man with the Golden Gun

The island is surrounded by huge mushroom-shaped rocks, protruding from the sea like fingers. With their foliage covering, the rocks look prehistoric; you almost expect to see pterodactyls flying about them. One of the series' most atmospheric moments happens when 007 (ROGER MOORE) is piloting his seaplane between these rock formations to the accompaniment of John Barry's score.

2. Venice in Moonraker

This unique and beautiful city is one of the finest 007 locales. *Moonraker* features the splendors of Venice to fine ef-

Did you know that?

James Bond has not only been fortunate enough to visit some of the most exotic locations in the world. He has also had the good fortune of perfect weather. *Not once* in the entire series has it ever rained.

fect, focusing on the Piazza San Marco and the many canals that traverse the city. Of course the recklessness we expect from a Bond film erupts in a speedboat chase along the canals and this almost destroys much of the city!

3. The Swiss Alps in On Her Majesty's Secret Service

Bond's antagonist Blofeld has a hideout, Piz Gloria, atop a peak in the Swiss Alps. Of all Bond villains he must have the best view and it certainly provides one of the best locations in a Bond film. The location used for Piz Gloria enabled exciting skiing and bobsled sequences to be filmed. The aerial shots of Bond (GEORGE LAZENBY) arrving at Piz Gloria by helicopter take your breath away. If you've never gone skiing in the Alps, this film will make you want to.

4. Iguacu Falls in Moonraker

Brazil's Iguacu Falls, one of the widest waterfalls in the world, is the setting for a motorboat chase that ends on a thrilling note with Bond (ROGER MOORE) hang gliding above the awe-inspiring drops. Like Phuket in *The Man with the Golden Gun*, the falls and surrounding jungle have a prehistoric look. The scene and the expansive landscape must be watched on widesreen!

5. The Beach in Dr. No

The Jamaican beach, which doubles for *Dr. No*'s private island, Crab Key, is the sort of tropical paradise that you only see in the movies. Although 007 has been on several tropical beaches in his day, this one in Jamaica stands out. It might be because this is where Ursula Andress prances around in that marvelous white bikini of hers! But whatever the case, this beach is definitely a place I would like to visit.

Honorable mention: the Bahamas in *Thunderball*; the Egyptian Pyramids in *The Spy Who Loved Me*; Vienna in *The Living Daylights*.

And for the record . . .

In the 19 James Bond films to date, 007 has visited or passed through the following locations (in chronological order):

Jamaica; Istanbul; Yugoslavia (passed through); Venice; Mexico; Miami; Switzerland; Kentucky; France; The Bahamas; Hong Kong; Tokyo; Spain; Switzerland (2nd visit); Cairo; Amsterdam; Las Vegas; New York; San Monique (fictional Caribbean island); New Orleans; Beirut; Hong Kong (2nd visit); Macau; Thailand; Phuket; Austria; Cairo (2nd visit); Sardinia; California; Venice (2nd visit); Rio de Janeiro; Outer Space; Spain (2nd visit); Cortina d'Ampezzo; Greece; Central America; India; Karl-Marx-Stadt; West Germany; Siberia; Paris; San Francisco; Gibraltar; Bratislava; Vienna; Tangiers; Afghanistan; Key West; Isthmus City (fictional Central American city); Russia; Monte Carlo; St. Petersburg; Puerto Rico; Cuba; Khyber Pass; Hamburg; Okinawa; Saigon; Bilbao; Azerbaijan; Baku; Kazakhstan; Istanbul (2nd visit).

Fallen Friends

It may have never rained on a James Bond film but 007 almost always has at least one "fallen friend" in each movie. This is a friend or ally of Bond who the baddies kill, usually in an original fashion. Whether Bond discovers the body after the fact, or the killing happens right in front of him, this is the moment the film generates some anger and remorse in the audience and in Bond and strengthens Bond's resolve to get the bad guys at all costs. I remember particularly these fallen friends:

1. Jill Masterson in Goldfinger

Bond (SEAN CONNERY) has just seduced and bedded Goldfinger's assistant Jill Masterson (SHIRLEY EATON). They are lying in his hotel bed, when Bond finds that the bottle of Dom Perignon '53, conveniently located beside the bed, has "lost its chill." So he gets up and walks over to the fridge to retrieve another. But instead, he receives a judo chop from Goldfinger's manservant, Odd Job (HAROLD SAKATA), to the back of the neck that knocks him out cold. When he revives, he stumbles back to the bedroom. Switching on the lights,

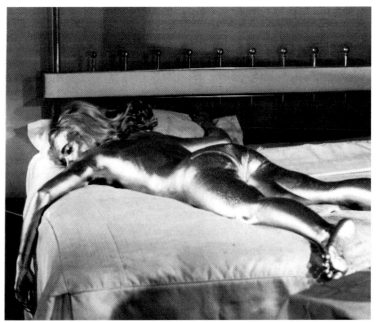

Jill (SHIRLEY EATON) receives "the Midas touch" in Goldfinger

he discovers the half-naked, dead body of Jill covered from head to toe in gold paint! Jill coated in gold has become perhaps the most lasting image of the series; a never-to-be-forgotten "fallen friend."

2. Kerim Bey in From Russia With Love

Istanbul Station Chief Kerim Bey (PEDRO ARMENDARIZ) has been an enormous help to Bond (SEAN CONNERY) on his mission to Turkey. Not only has he willingly assisted 007, but he has done so in such a charismatic way that Bond is truly taken with him and they have become good friends. Kerim Bey is as close to a father figure as we've seen Bond have (outside of M), so the shock is genuine when Bond finds Kerim's murdered body on board the Orient Express. It is a real look of pain on Bond's face at that rare moment, one of the few when Bond's emotion is seen on screen.

3. Saunders in The Living Daylights

James Bond (TIMOTHY DALTON) and Vienna Station Chief Saunders (THOMAS WHEATLEY) have not exactly seen eye to eye for most of the film. Saunders has railed against 007's propensity to not play by the rules, which causes considerable friction between them. Finally, after much coaxing, Saunders has grudgingly agreed to find the information that Bond needs. They meet at the counter of the Prater Café in Vienna, where Saunders delivers information on Soviet General Koskov and his girlfriend Kara that Bond needs. Saunders leaves the café, having received Bond's heartfelt

Did you know that?

Six British Secret Service agents have been killed while assisting James Bond: Kerim Bey in *From Russia With Love*; Paula in *Thunderball*; Shaun in *On Her Majesty's Secret Service*; Vijay in *Octopussy*; Tibbet in *A View To A Kill*; Saunders in *The Living Daylights*.

"Thanks." Bond is well aware that the man went against his policy of playing by the book to get the information to him, and Bond's appreciation is real. What Bond and Saunders don't know is that the malicious Necros (ANDREAS WISNIEWSKI) is waiting outside. He controls a remote device rigged to move the glass sliding doors at the café's entrance. Necros pushes a button on the remote control as Saunders passes through that causes the doors to race shut. They slam into him and, although we don't see it on film, slice him in two. With the screaming of terrified customers, Bond jumps up and runs over to investigate. As he kneels over Saunders' body, Bond conveys a helplessness that we've not seen before. Yet, when a balloon floats over to Bond, he picks it up and reads on it the words "Smiert Spionam." (That's Russian for "Death to Spies.") The words enrage him. He pops the balloon in anger, well aware that Saunders' death was no accident and that he will make the perpetrators of it pay. A chilling moment.

4. Paris Carver in Tomorrow Never Dies

Bond's ex-flame Paris Carver (TERI HATCHER), now the
wife of the devilish Elliot Carver, pays the ultimate price
for helping her ex-beau as Bond (PIERCE BROSNAN) discovers
when he returns to his Hamburg hotel suite. The TV is on
and shows a news reporter stating that Paris Carver, wife of
media mogul Elliot Carver, has been found dead in a Hamburg hotel. Bond walks by the TV and sees Paris lying dead
on his bed. Kneeling over her body and overcome with
emotion, he stiffens when he hears the news report con-

*Bond (PIERCE BROSNAN) bids farewell to Paris (TERI HATCHER)
in* Tomorrow Never Dies

tinue that Mrs. Carver's body was found along with the body of an unidentified man. 007 realizes that that man is supposed to be him. His suspicion is verified when the voice of the mysterious Dr. Kaufman (VINCENT SCHIAVELLI) announces he is pointing a gun at Bond's head. It is true that Mrs. Carver's body is found with a dead man, but unfortunately for Dr. Kaufman, that man won't be James Bond.

5. *Aki in You Only Live Twice*

Aki (AKIKO WAKABAYASHI), able agent of the Japanese Secret Service, assists Bond (SEAN CONNERY) throughout *You Only Live Twice*, both in and out of bed. They are sleeping together in their hut at a Ninja training base that a SPECTRE assassin has infiltrated. The assassin sneaks onto the ceiling rafters of the hut and quietly un-ravels a string, letting it down until one end touches Bond's lips. He then takes out a vial of poison and pours the liquid down the string, where it slowly seeps downward. As the poison is about to drip onto Bond's lips, he turns in his sleep. Unfortunately, Aki turns with him and the poison touches her lips instead. She instantly begins to convulse and Bond awakens. He hears the assassin above, pulls out his Walther and kills the man with one shot. But it is too late for Aki.

Honorable mention: Corinne in *Moonraker*; Vijay in *Octopussy;* Della in *Licence To Kill*.

Other Gems

Despite all the categories in this book, some scenes that I love don't fit into any of them. Yet a book about the best moments in the Bond series wouldn't be complete without including these scenes. So here are 5 assorted gems:

1. *Bond confronts General Orlov in Octopussy*

007 (ROGER MOORE) and rogue Soviet General Orlov (STEPHEN BERKOFF) are in the back of a storage car on Octopussy's circus train. Bond has discovered that Orlov has secretly planted an atomic bomb in the base of a circus cannon soon to be delivered via rail to a U.S. Air Force base in West Germany. Pointing his Walther PPK directly at Orlov's head, Bond demands to know Orlov's reasons behind this mad act and tells him in no uncertain terms that's he's going to "stop that train." The forcefulness and seriousness behind Roger Moore's tone is electrifying. It may be his best moment as Bond. An unsuspecting Soviet soldier enters their car and witnesses the general staring down Bond's Walther, but he doesn't live to report what he sees. He is killed by a quick bullet to the head from 007. Chilling.

2. *Bond face to face with General Pushkin in The Living Daylights*

Reminiscent of Bond's confrontation with Orlov in *Octopussy*, this scene is no less effective. Soviet General Pushkin (JOHN RHYS-DAVIES) enters his Tangiers hotel room. Holding a bouquet of flowers for his wife, he finds his wife extremely shaken. He soon discovers why. James Bond (TIMOTHY DALTON) is hiding behind the door with his silenced Walther PPK at the ready. 007 orders the general to sit in a chair at the foot of the bed; his terrified wife looks on. The general sits, then Bond pushes the chair over, so the general is knocked to the bed. His wife jumps up to help him, until she freezes when Bond turns his gun on her. He redirects the gun to Pushkin's head and demands to know about "Smiert Spionam," a supposed Soviet operation to kill western agents. Pushkin tries to talk his way out of his predicament, while secretly touching an alarm-button on his watch, that will alert Pushkin's bodyguard, who is sitting in the hallway. But Bond notices him hit the button and slams his gun into Pushkin's side in reprisal. He also collars Pushkin's wife, and tears the top off her nightgown. Having done this, he runs to the side of the door as it opens. The sight of the half-naked Mrs. Pushkin shocks the guard that he is distracted long enough for 007 to bang his gun into the man's head, which knocks him out cold. Bond orders Mrs. Pushkin into the bathroom, while he continues interrogating the general. This taut, tense and brutal scene may be Bond being seen at his toughest and meanest. Certainly it showcases Dalton at his best and is something that Ian Fleming might have enjoyed.

3. *Bond battles Mr. Wint and Mr. Kidd in Diamonds Are Forever*

Towards the end of the movie, Bond (SEAN CONNERY) and Tiffany Case (JILL ST. JOHN) are enjoying a quiet moment on the sun deck of their luxurious cabin aboard a cruise liner. Two waiters interrupt their peace when they wheel a large buffet table into the room. The two waiters are none other than Blofeld's smirking assassins, Mr. Wint (BRUCE GLOVER) and Mr. Kidd (PUTTER SMITH). Unfortunately Bond doesn't know this, because he's never seen them. Earlier in the film, from behind Wint had knocked Bond unconscious. But Bond had smelled Wint's pungent after-shave that lingered on him and he remembered it. Bond and Tiffany sit at the table and the two assassins begin to prepare the meal. We see Kidd place a time-bomb beneath a phony *bombe surprise* cake. As he does this, Wint opens a bottle of wine and hands the cork to 007. Bond sniffs the cork and comments, "That's rather potent. Not the cork. Your after-shave." His suspicions grow. He sips the wine and adds, "but the wine is quite excellent. Although for such a grand meal, I rather expected a claret." A growing-nervous-by-the-second Mr. Wint apologizes, "Unfortunately our cellar is rather poorly stocked with clarets." Bond hardens and says, "Mouton Rothschild is a claret. And I've smelt that after-shave before and both times I've smelt a rat." Mr. Kidd jumps into action, lights two skewers of shish-kebab on a flame and lunges at Bond just as Wint pulls out a garrote and wraps it around Bond's neck. But Bond acts swiftly as well. He breaks the bottle of Mouton Rothschild and hurls the liquid at Mr. Kidd, which feeds the already flaming shish-kebab, and Kidd turns into a torch. This enrages Mr. Wint, who tightens the garrote around Bond's neck. Tiffany, wanting to save Bond, picks up the *bombe surprise* and flings it at Wint. It sails over his head and crashes to the floor, exposing the ticking time-bomb. Summoning all of his strength, Bond flips Wint over his head and to the floor, after which 007 scrambles for the time-bomb. He ties it firmly to the tails of Wint's tuxedo and shoves Wint over the side of the sun deck. The time-bomb explodes and sends what's left of Wint into the ocean. Bond glances over the side and says, "He certainly left with his tail between his legs."

4. Escape from the Wavekrest in Licence To Kill

A sequence towards the middle of the film, although not just a chase, a fight, a shootout, or a stunt, may just be the best action sequence of the series. The thrill derives from it being a combination of all these four elements. Bond (TIMO-THY DALTON) sneaks onto drug runner Milton Krest's boat, the Wavekrest, where he hopes to find information to help him locate drug lord Franz Sanchez. He finds Sanchez's girl-friend, Lupe (TALISA SOTO), sleeping in a cabin and wakes her by putting a knife to her throat. He demands to know where Sanchez is. She can't tell him. At that moment Bond is dis-tracted by something he sees outside the porthole: The body of his friend Sharkey is hanging from a fish-hook on a fishing boat that has come up alongside the Wavekrest. The image has Bond seething and he says to her, "You'd better find yourself a new lover." Is this where the fun begins? Bond comes up on deck and grasps a spear gun, which he fires at one of the divers who killed Sharkey as he comes aboard. 007 then jumps into the water. A small sea-plane has landed and is floating near the Wavekrest. It has been unloading a cache of cocaine into the Wavekrest's underwater probe, the Sentinel. Bond intercepts the Sentinel as it is hauled back towards the Wavekrest, opens it up and starts slashing at the cocaine packages. This brings divers from the Wavekrest

Did you know that?

Ten James Bond movies have ended with him floating on or in the water: *Dr. No* (on a boat in the Caribbean); *From Russia With Love* (in a gondola in Venice); *You Only Live Twice* (on a rubber raft in the Sea of Japan); *Diamonds Are Forever* (aboard a cruise-liner); *The Man with the Golden Gun* (on a sailing junk in the South China Sea); *The Spy Who Loved Me* (in a floating escape pod in the Mediterranean); *For Your Eyes Only* (swimming in the Mediterranean); *Octopussy* (on a boat in India); *Licence To Kill* (in a pool in Isthmus City); *Tomorrow Never Dies* (on the debris of Carver's sunken stealth ship in the South China Sea).

after him. They converge on Bond underwater and fire spears at him. Bond fends the attackers off with his fists and legs, and at the last moment steals one of their spear guns. Looking up, he sees the sea-plane taxiing across the water and fires a spear—which stays attached by cord to the gun—at the plane's landing gear. The spear catches in the landing gear and as the plane picks up speed for takeoff, Bond is pulled up out of the water and away from his attackers. 007 "water-skis" at high speed—without the advantage of skis!—behind the plane with Krest's men behind him in speedboats firing machine guns at him. Bond swings himself closer to the plane and throws himself at the landing gear, grabbing onto it just as the plane lifts off. The pilot of the plane swirls the plane around to try and dislodge Bond. But Bond hangs on and it doesn't work. 007 works his way into the back of the plane and crawls behind the bags of drug money that fill the plane. He comes up stealthily behind the co-pilot, pulls the emergency latch on the plane's side door and door and co-pilot hurtle down to the sea. The pilot turns on Bond and begins firing his revolver at him, but Bond shields himself with one of the tightly packed moneybags. Moving in on the pilot, 007 bashes him with the money bag and they fight furiously. A well-placed and final kick to the pilot's jaw knocks him out. Bond seizes the controls, steadies the plane, and flies away as Krest watches from his boat below in disbelief.

5. The Stare in Goldfinger

A fraction of a moment that resonates with me every time I see it involves Auric Goldfinger (GERT FROBE) and his absolute love and lust for gold. Having heard him describing his lust, we finally see it for ourselves in one painstakingly profound moment. Goldfinger has just left 007 (SEAN CONNERY) handcuffed to an atom bomb inside the vault at Fort Knox. The bomb, set to explode shortly, will contaminate the U.S. gold supply for 58 years. Pleased that his plan has gone so well, Goldfinger prepares to leave the vault. But he has to take one last stare at the gold. You see, this isn't just any gold. These gold bars, stacked high, are the shiniest, the most glistening, the most beautiful gold Auric Goldfinger or you or I have ever laid eyes upon. And as he realizes what his atom bomb is going to contaminate, the look of pain and regret that he gives it is telling. In that one instant you almost believe that Goldfinger wants to run back into the vault and call the whole thing off! Of course, he quickly composes himself and has the vault closed. Yet that stare says more about his character than any other scene.

Last Lines

A James Bond movie can't just fade out. There has to be a funny line to close it out and that gives the audience one last chuckle before they head for the exits.

The following five are the most memorable:

1. Goldfinger

James Bond (SEAN CONNERY) and Pussy Galore (HONOR BLACKMAN) have parachute-landed somewhere in a forest in Kentucky. A military search helicopter appears overhead, so Pussy stands up and waves her jacket to get its attention. But before she can succeed, Bond yanks her down to the ground and pulls her into his arms, while simultaneously covering them with the chute. Closing in on her, he says, "This is no time to be rescued."

2. The Spy Who Loved Me

James Bond (ROGER MOORE) and KGB agent Triple X, Anya Amasova (BARBARA BACH) have fled the sinking Atlantis, evil Karl Stromberg's seaborne hideout, in a floating escape pod. The pod is equipped with a luxurious white circular bed, which Bond and Anya waste no time getting into. Scarcely have their amorous activities started, than their pod is discovered by a Royal Navy vessel. M, Q, the British Minister of Defence and General Gogol of the KGB happen to be aboard. These gentlemen peer over the ship's side into the escape pod's window and see Bond and Anya "debriefing" each other in the bed. Anya notices that they are being watched and alerts 007, while they pull the sheets up over their bodies. M (BERNARD LEE), disgusted, moans, "007." General Gogol (WALTER GOTELL), shocked, cries, "Triple X!" The Minister of Defence (GEOFFREY KEEN), furious, yells, "Bond! What the hell do you think you're doing?!" Bond pauses before saying, "Just keeping the British end up, sir."

Anya (BARBARA BACH) helps Bond (ROGER MOORE) keep his end up in The Spy Who Loved Me

3. *The World Is Not Enough*

Somewhere in Istanbul, James Bond (PIERCE BROSNAN) and Dr. Christmas Jones (DENISE RICHARDS) lie in bed together. They have just saved the city from nuclear destruction and have been celebrating their accomplishment, topping off their celebration by having sex. Bond says to Christmas, "I was wrong about you." "Yeah, how so?" she asks. "I thought Christmas comes only once a year," he replies.

4. Moonraker

James Bond (ROGER MOORE) and Dr. Holly Goodhead (LOIS CHILES) have saved planet Earth and are floating around inside the Moonraker space shuttle that will return them to Earth. Weightless from the zero-gravity and wrapped in the sheets in which they have just made love, Bond says to Goodhead, "I think it's time to go home." "James. Take me around the world one more time," she begs. "Why not?" he replies.

5. On Her Majesty's Secret Service

Something of a black sheep choice, because this is the only Bond film that doesn't end happy and the film's final line reflects this. Blofeld's assistant, Irma Bunt, has murdered Bond's bride Tracy (DIANA RIGG). Bond (GEORGE LAZENBY) sits slumped in his Aston Martin caressing his wife's body, when a police officer pokes his head into Bond's car to see what has happened. Bond looks up and says, "It's alright. She's having a rest. We'll be moving on shortly. You see we have all the time in the world."

Thus ends the journey showcasing the best of the James Bond series. But perhaps the best is yet to come. For if there is one thing certain in this world, it is that James Bond will return . . .

in

Die Another Day.

Bond (SEAN CONNERY) kisses Kissy (MIE HAMA) at the end of
You Only Live Twice

About the Author

MICHAEL DI LEO is a native New Yorker and a 1989 graduate of Utica College of Syracuse University. A Bond fan since the age of 4, he works as a property manager in Manhattan and currently lives on Long Island with his wife Elisa and daughter Gianna. This is his first book.